NEVER BEYOND HOPE

HOW GOD TOUCHES &

USES IMPERFECT PEOPLE

J. I. PACKER
AND CAROLYN NYSTROM

InterVarsity Press
Downers Grove, Illinois

InterVarsity Press
P.O. Box 1400, Downers Grove, IL 60515-1426
World Wide Web: www.ivpress.com
E-mail: mail@ivpress.com

InterVarsity Press® is the book-publishing division of InterVarsity Christian Fellowship/ USA®, a student movement active on campus at hundreds of universities, colleges and schools of nursing in the United States of America, and a member movement of the International Fellowship of Evangelical Students. For information about local and regional activities, write Public Relations Dept., InterVarsity Christian Fellowship/USA, 6400 Schroeder Rd., P.O. Box 7895, Madison, WI 53707-7895, or visit the IVCF website at <www.intervarsity.org>.

Design: Cindy Kiple

Images: Stephen Wilkes/Getty Images

ISBN 0-8308-3272-6

Printed in the United States of America ∞

Library of Congress Cataloging-in-Publication Data

Packer, J. I. (James Innell)
  Never beyond hope: how God touches and uses imperfect people
/ J.I.
  Packer and Carolyn Nystrom.
      p. cm.
  Originally published: c2000.
  Includes bibliographical references.
  ISBN 0-8308-3272-6 (pbk.: alk paper)
  1. Hope—Religious aspects—Christianity. 2. Bible—Biography. I.
Nystrom, Carolyn. II. Title.
BV4638.P33 2005
234'.25—dc22
                                                                        2004025528

P   16   15   14   13   12   11   10   9   8   7   6   5   4   3   2
Y   16   15   14   13   12   11   10   09   08   07   06   05

CONTENTS

TO THE READER

We composed this book together, and we would like to tell you how and why. Carolyn Nystrom heard J. I. Packer speak on Samson and asked if she might write up what he said. Dr. Packer told her that he had in store other messages exploring the Samson theme, namely, God blessing and using flawed human beings to further his plans. One thing led to another, and we agreed to have a go at sharing this material, Carolyn Nystrom transcribing, editing, providing study guidance, giving devotional leads and crafting the book overall. What you hold in your hand is the end product of this combined operation.

J. I. Packer's material, apart from the introduction, expands addresses given in public. No attempt has been made to tone down his preaching style and homiletical rhetoric. When you find an "I" reference in the book, then, it is J. I. Packer speaking. Carolyn Nystrom's expertise appears in the study questions, the prayer suggestions and the writing directives. Together we say with emphasis that only those who, individually or as a group, work through these applicatory exercises will benefit fully from what we have done.

We urge that whether or not you are a regular journal keeper, you use a separate notebook for the writing. The reason is that if you start doing it on the blank pages and half-pages of the book itself, you will not have enough space to finish it there.

All of us, one way or another, are problem people, and the divine grace celebrated in these pages is something that you, like us, need at a very deep level. May this book that comes from our hearts go to your heart, and may God touch your life through it.

J. I. Packer
Carolyn Nystrom

Introduction: God's Gift of Hope

"May the God of hope fill you with all joy and peace as you trust in him, so that you may overflow with hope by the power of the Holy Spirit" (Rom 15:13). So wrote Paul to the Christians at Rome as he rounded off the argument of his greatest letter. I have been a believer for more than half a century, but only recently have I appreciated how pastorally profound Paul's prayer was—and is.

As I write this, the year-long hopes of a peaceful settlement in Northern Ireland have just collapsed, and a revenge massacre of farmers in Kosovo has just shown that hopes of speedy return to ordered peace in that land of agony must, for the present, be shelved. Observers in both countries are dwelling on the renewed sense of wretchedness, numbing for some and nightmarish for others, that these turns of events have brought. Nor is it any wonder that such feelings should rise, for the death of hope has a killing effect on human minds and hearts.

While there's life there's hope, we say, but the deeper truth is that only while there's hope is there life. Take away hope, and life, with all its fascinating variety of opportunities and experiences, reduces to mere existence—uninteresting, ungratifying, bleak, drab and repellent, a burden and a pain. People without hope often express their sense of reality and their feelings about themselves by saying they wish they were dead, and sometimes they make attempts on their own life.

Years ago the wife of a man I knew as a student published a testimony titled "Made Redundant." It began like this: "I shall never forget Francis' face as he walked through our front door that evening. . . . It was quite gray and utterly defeated." Terminated without warning, Francis (she wrote) was then rebuffed everywhere. "He was willing to do any work at all . . . but no one wanted him. It hurt me to see a man usually so full of vigor and ideas just silently helping me with the housework or sitting aimlessly staring into space." How many couples in the Western world have known that experience during the past quarter century! Then, while the family's needs were being covered at a prayer meeting, into his mind had come a plan for starting a small business. When his wife got back, she found him smiling. "While we had been praying he had felt a change come over him. Hope had sprung up within him and with it decisions, ideas, action." Exactly! That is what hope does for you. The plan proved sound, and the crisis was surmounted. Her article ended thus:

> I do not know why Francis lost his job. I do not know why he is doing well now. But I do know that I can trust God. I do know that he will provide shelter and warmth and clothing and food. And he can give, even in the blackest moments, hope; and after faith and love, hope is one of his most precious gifts to mankind.

No one ever spoke a truer word.

The fact of the matter is that we human beings are so made that we live very much in our own fancied future. This is not a policy decision but simply the way we are. To look forward, to dream of happy things to come, to want what is good to continue and what is bad to end, and to long for a future that is better than the past is as natural as breathing. As Alexander Pope said in his pompous way: "Hope springs eternal in the human breast: / Man never *is*, but always *to be* blest." To be sure, there are individuals, families, human groups and entire cultures with pessimistic mindsets, as if they think it wisdom not to hope for anything good, but as such an attitude is not cheerful, so it is not natural, any more than atheism is. Both are the result of disillusionment. As atheisms stem from being disappointed and hurt in some way by the theism of theists, or by its exponents, so pessimisms flow from the shattering of natural optimism. Hope generates energy, enthusiasm and excitement; lack of hope breeds only apathy and inertia. So for fully developed, as distinct from partly diminished, humanness, there needs to be hope in our hearts.

If we come to think or feel (often we are not quite rational about this) that we have nothing to hope for and can only expect things to get worse in the future, inevitably we grow depressed and, to a degree, desperate. We may try to hide our condition, but the unfocused rage, fury and hatred of life that we feel work like acid, dissolving all other feelings into purest bitterness. Hopelessness is thus at the root of many of today's psychological disorders, as the growing frequency of random killings and suicides among us seems to show. And even when hopelessness is only fitful and intermittent, a mood that possesses until it passes, it still makes us feel alone, afraid and paralyzed for action. We find that we cannot make decisions nor bring ourselves to do things. Our sense of self-worth dissolves into self-doubt, self-distrust and self-dislike; confidence is swallowed up by despair. We find ourselves in a tunnel that has no light at the end of it, only deeper darkness and eventually a blank wall.

When the philosopher Immanuel Kant said that one of life's three basic questions is, What may we hope for? he was right. Where then shall we look for an answer to that question? To politics and the socio-economic engineering that goes with it? Hardly. Politicians know that we all need hope and indeed ache for it, so their rhetoric is always upbeat. But to us of the old West (I mean Europe, including Britain; North America, including Canada; and Australasia, including New Zealand) politicians' promises and predictions cannot but sound hollow, for we see clearly that they have never fulfilled the hopes placed in them, and we are sadly sure that they never will. The past century's national and international politics, along with global economic development, educational advances, wealth creation, technological triumphs, medical marvels, radio and television in every home, and the coming of the computer, has instead eroded hopes rather than gratified them because of the new possibilities of distress and disaster that these changes have brought. Political, technological and business activity have combined to make our planet's prospects for the third millennium distinctly ominous.

The twentieth century opened in optimism. The ruling assumption in the old West was that we are all basically good and wise, and advancing Christian civilization would soon make the kingdom of God, understood as universal neighbor love, a global reality. A periodical called *The Christian Century* was founded to channel these hopes and chronicle their fulfillment; it still exists, but its title now seems woefully inept. We have experienced the renewing of global barbarism in two World Wars and in the careers of power-crazy, money-mad tribalists and the genocidal doings of dictators. We cringe at the profiteering of the world's big businesses as they pollute and rape the environment, destroy the ozone layer and destabilize the climate. We mourn our Western drift from Christian and moral moorings into relativism, pluralism, secularism and hedonism. We exist amidst escalations of the armaments trade and the ability to devastate the world with nuclear weapons. These events and more all tell us that the twentieth was not a particularly Christian century. Furthermore, these twentieth-century developments ensure that many thoughtful people entered the twenty-first century in fear rather than in hope, wondering how far the educated, affluent and technologically equipped decadence of the West will go and what sort of a world awaits our grandchildren. It can be fairly said that Marxist utopianism, with its collectivist frame, has failed and is not likely to be tried anywhere again. As the third millennium opens, any who expect that politicians' and generals' playing of the power game and business leaders' playing of the profit game will generate global peace and prosperity have buried their heads very deep in the sands. No realistic hope of better things to come can be drawn from the ways of the modern world.

What follows? Is there nothing good to hope for at all? There is, but we must seek this good hope outside the socio-politico-economic process. And this, by the grace of God, we may do. For God the Creator, who designed us, sustains us and knows our hearts, never intended that humans should live without hope. On the contrary, he makes himself known in the gospel as "the God of hope" (Paul's phrase, as we saw). There he invites all the world to receive "Christ Jesus our hope" (1 Tim 1:1) and accept renovation by "Christ in you, the hope of glory" (Col 1:27). As God the Father is a God of hope, so his incarnate Son, Jesus of Nazareth, crucified, risen, reigning and returning, is a messenger, means and mediator of hope; and the Bible, "God's Word written" as the Anglican doctrinal standard, the Thirty-nine Articles, describes it, is from Genesis to Revelation a book of hope. The first recorded divine promise, that the woman's seed would crush the serpent's head, was a word of hope in the Garden of Eden (Gen 3:15), and the last recorded promise of Jesus, "I am coming soon" (Rev 22:20), was a word of hope for churches facing persecution. Hebrews 11:1 defines faith in terms of hope ("Now faith is being sure of what we hope for"). Hope, the guaranteed expectation enabling believers to look forward with joy, is in truth one of the great themes of Christianity and one of the supreme gifts of God.

What the Bible tells us about hope, in a nutshell, is this: Humans were originally created in fellowship with God so that we might exalt and enjoy him forever, first for a probationary period in this world and then in a place of "eternal pleasures" (Ps 16:11) that is off the map of this space-time universe. When sin infected our race, disrupting this fellowship, robbing us all of the hope of heaven and bringing us all under the threat of hell, our Creator acted to form a forgiven and reborn interracial human race, namely, the church, a community that should enjoy humankind's original destiny and more through sovereign divine grace and personal faith in our Lord Jesus Christ. So believers in every age should live in the knowledge that they are God's adopted children and heirs of what is spoken of as his glory, his city and his kingdom. They should know that Jesus Christ, who out of love gave his life for the church inclusively (Eph 5:25) and for each future believer personally (Gal 2:20), is now with them individually by his Spirit (Mt 28:20), to care for them daily as a shepherd for his sheep (Jn 10:2-4, 11-25) and to strengthen them constantly according to their need (Phil 4:13; 2 Tim 4:17), and that he will finally take them from this world to see and share the heavenly bliss that is already his (Jn 14:1-3, 17:24; Rom 8:17). With Paul, therefore, they should "eagerly await through the Spirit the righteousness for which we hope" (Gal 5:5)—that is, the full fruit of being fully accepted by God, or as New Living Translation puts it, "eagerly wait to receive everything promised to us who are right with God through faith." The Christian identity is that not only of a believer but of a hoper too.

We can now clearly see that the word *hope* signifies two distinct, though related, realities. Objectively, it means the divinely guaranteed prospect before us; subjectively, it means the activity or habit of looking forward to the day when what is promised will become ours in actual enjoyment. It is thus quite distinct from optimism. Optimism hopes for the best without any guarantee of its arriving and is often no more than whistling in the dark. Christian hope, by contrast, is faith looking ahead to the fulfillment of the promises of God, as when the Anglican burial service inters the corpse "in sure and certain hope of the Resurrection to eternal life, through our Lord Jesus Christ." Optimism is a wish without a warrant; Christian hope is a certainty, guaranteed by God himself. Optimism reflects ignorance as to whether good things will ever actually come. Christian hope expresses knowledge that each day of his life, and every moment beyond it, the believer can say with truth, on the basis of God's own commitment, that the best is still to come.

The mindset of Christian hopers is much decried today. It clashes with the proud this-worldliness of our sophisticated and materialistic culture, and that of itself stirs resentment. Marxists oppose it because they think the hope (delusive, on their view) of "pie in the sky when you die" makes for passivity and keeps the masses from taking revolutionary action for social change. Some psychological counselors are against it because they see it as a form of escapism, keeping people from facing life's realities. The truth is, however, that Christian hoping, by virtue of its object (the guaranteed, never-ending generosity of God), calls forth love, joy, zeal, initiative and devoted action, so that, as C. S. Lewis put it, those who have done most for the present world have been those who thought most of the next.

Paul himself in Romans displays the reality of this. He presents Abraham as a model of justifying faith because he believed a promise of God shaping his future that at the time seemed too good to be true. "Against all hope, Abraham in hope believed . . . being fully persuaded that God had power to do what he had promised" (Rom 4:1-3, 16-22). Describing the life of those justified by faith, he writes: "We rejoice in the hope of the glory of God" (5:2; see also 12:12, "Be joyful in hope"). Having said that we long for the promised redemption of our bodies, he continues: "For in [or with, or for, or by] this hope we are saved. But hope that is seen is no hope at all. Who hopes for what he already has? But if we hope for what we do not yet have, we wait for it patiently" (8:24–25). Here he is telling his readers to hope thoughtfully, intentionally, understandingly and tenaciously for the transformational completing of the salvation that, relationally and positionally, they have already received. We learn from Paul that as we have been saved in one sense, so we shall be saved in another. Salvation is both now and not yet. We should thank God for it in the former sense, in which it became ours upon our believing (1:16, 6:17–18, 22-23; 11:11, 14), while we await its coming in the latter sense, confident that every day brings it nearer (13:11). Then in 15:5 Paul tells us strikingly that "everything that was written in the past"—that is, all of what we call the Old Testament—"was written to teach us"—he means, us Christian believers—"so that through endurance and encouragement of the Scriptures we might have hope." And in 15:13, as we saw, he prays that the "God of hope" will enable his readers to "overflow with hope" as they take these things to heart.

Does Paul's emphasis on hope, which so evidently expresses the motions of his own heart (the "we" and the "us" in the passages quoted show that), reduce at all the energy and intensity of his apostolic labors? Not in the least, rather the reverse. He writes to the Romans as one who, having evangelized the Mediterranean world from Jerusalem to the Adriatic coast, now plans to visit Rome on his way to a mission in Spain (see Rom 15:15–28). He was perhaps the most enterprising missionary the world has ever seen and was certainly entitled to say as a simple matter of fact, "I worked harder than all of them—yet not I, but the grace of God that was with me" (1 Cor 15:10). His hope included not only his personal resurrection and a joyful eternity with Christ (Phil 1:20–23; 3:8–14) but also the raising up of a believing community among non-Jews everywhere under his ministry.

Paul was a tireless pioneer in traveling and preaching to make this happen. Hope of seeing the fulfillment of God's plan did not lead him to relax in the task but gave him strength to go on with it, just as God's plan to bring him bodily into the realm of resurrection spurred him forward "to take hold of that for which Christ Jesus took hold of me . . . one thing I do; forgetting what is behind and straining toward what is ahead, I press on toward the goal to win the prize for which God has called me heavenward in Christ Jesus" (Phil 3:12–14). In spiritual life and ministry Paul's hope did for him what athletes hope training and lifting weights will do for them physically: it supplied strength and enhanced performance. So it should be with all of us. That leads us to the next point, which has to do with our own performance.

A truth of which healthy growing Christians become more and more aware is that God is transcendently great and the human individual by comparison is infinitely insignificant. God, we realize, can get on very well without any of us. So it should give us an overwhelming sense of privilege that not only has he made, loved and saved us but also he takes us as his working partners for advancing his plans. Thus Paul can call his colleagues and himself "Christ's ambassadors" and "God's fellow workers" (2 Cor 3:20; 6:1), and tell us all to see ourselves in our own sphere as servants, ministers and workmen of God. Just as fifty years ago people felt it gave them great dignity to work for Winston Churchill because of who he was, so we should derive a great sense of dignity from the knowledge of being called to do things for God. And none of us is excluded, for Scripture shows God using the oddest, rawest, most lopsided and flawed of his children to further his work, at the same time as he carries on his sanctifying strategy for getting them into better moral and spiritual shape. This is a fact of enormous encouragement to sensitive souls who feel they are not fit to serve him. In this book we shall see God dealing with Samson the womanizer, Jacob the cheat, hot-tempered Nehemiah, diffident Mrs. Manoah, bossy noisy Martha and quiet passive Mary, Jonah the pig-headed patriot, Thomas the stupid-smart professional pessimist, and impulsive, warm-hearted, unstable Simon Peter. We shall note how God blessed and used these people even as he led them forward out of bondage to their own defects into truer godliness than they knew before. The knowledge that this is God's way with his flawed friends is here offered in the human hope that it will stir up divine hope of being useful to God in the hearts of some who hitherto have thought themselves too faulty for this dignity.

Hope is a tender plant, easily crushed and extinguished, and every believer must budget for having to battle for it. Many are the moments of disappointment and frustration, when we say and feel that things are hopeless, and all hope is gone. Disappointment will then lead us, if we let it, down the slippery slope through desolation and distress into depression and despair. The speeches of traumatized Job as he sat among the ashes, sick, bewildered and hurting in his mind as well as his body, express the death of hope in classic terms. "My days . . . come to an end without hope" (Job 7:6). "As water wears away stones and torrents wash away the soil, so you (God!) destroy man's hope" (14:18–19). "If the only home I hope for is the grave . . . where then is my hope? Who can see any hope for me?" (17:13–15). "He (God!) uproots my hope like a tree" (19:10). Living with the assumption that the godly would be materially enriched every time, and before the revelation of the hope of glory with Christ beyond this world, Job—though finally restored in material terms (42:10)—could receive no basis for hope from God other than: trust me to know what I'm doing, which is the message conveyed to him by God's review of some of the cosmic glories and wonderful living creatures he has made (see chaps. 38—41). But Chris-tians know more than Job knew, and Peter sets before us resources for the reviving of hope in our hearts whenever it is threatened. This is the passage: it is worth its weight in gold.

> Praise be to the God and Father of our Lord Jesus Christ! In his great mercy he has given us new birth into a living hope through the resurrection of Jesus Christ from the dead, and into an inheritance that can never perish, spoil or fade—kept in heaven for you, who through faith are shielded by God's power until the coming of the salvation that is ready to be revealed in the last time. In this you greatly rejoice, though now for a little while you may have had to suffer grief in all kinds of trials. These have come so that your faith—of greater worth than gold, which perishes even though refined by fire—may be proved genuine and may result in praise, glory and honor when Jesus Christ is revealed. Though you have not seen him you love him; and even though you do not see him

now, you believe in him and are filled with an inexpressible and glorious joy, for you are receiving the goal of your faith, the salvation of your souls. (1 Pet 1:3-9)

Do we need hope? Yes. May Christians hope? Yes. Are we ever beyond hope? No. Is the greatness of our hope an index of the graciousness of God? Yes. Does our hope of salvation bring joy, energy, faithfulness and a desire to be of use to God? Yes, yes, yes, yes. May we hope that God will use us each day to his glory, even though we are not as yet perfectly sanctified? Yes. Is this glorious good news? Yes.

Good hoping to you!—or as some say, here's hoping!—hoping as a way of life, hoping as a source of strength and hoping as a fountain of joy in the heart from which praise and prayer will flow out continually.

Is that the last thing I have to say? Not quite.

I think you know that evil is abroad in God's world: cunning, malicious, destructive evil, resourceful and implacable, headed up by a corrupted angel whom Scripture calls Satan (a Hebrew word meaning "the adversary" or "hostile opponent"). I think you know that Satan is here and now pursuing you personally, since by committing yourself to Jesus Christ you have lined up against him. By walking into the ongoing conflict between the Creator and the corrupter, which you did when you enlisted on the Lord's side, you have ensured that, willy-nilly, you will be living the rest of your life in a state of spiritual warfare. I think you know that not having managed to keep you from faith, Satan will do his damnedest (I use that word with precision for that which expresses and induces God's condemnation) to keep you from healthy growth in Christ and usefulness to him in work and witness. This means that Satan will labor to divert you from the paths of holiness and hope. And I think I know that some of you who read these words have already, deep down, caved in to Satan with regard to hope, so that the joy-giving, life-enhancing, energy-generating power of hope of which Paul and Peter speak is something you know little about. Please think with me for a moment as to how that might be changed.

To stifle hope as a habit of mind and heart Satan exploits both our inbuilt weaknesses of character and our acquired defects of attitude and behavior that testify to bad and failed relationships in our past. Thus some of us have a temperament that is naturally gloomy and melancholic (the old word for depressive), so that self-absorption and self-pity, feeling beached and abandoned, and expecting the worst come naturally to us, as they did to Eeyore in the saga of Winnie-the-Pooh. Some of us are burdened with a crushing sense of shyness and incompetence (clumsiness; slowness; lack of beauty, brains, brawn and brightness), so that we feel diffident and inferior and run scared, afraid of being caught out in some folly we failed to notice. Some of us bear the scars of pain we cannot forget and damage we cannot repair (from bad parenting, bullying, relational breakdown, sexual and substance abuse, and so on). Guilty memories keep shame and self-contempt alive in some of our hearts. Feeling imprisoned in a sick and wasting body, or a loveless home, or a soul-destroying routine encourages us to resent our very existence as a total misery. Emotional exhaustion over any length of time leaves us feeling, as a man once said to me, that our faith is as fragile as tissue paper, and hoping positively for anything is simply beyond us. Satan is a master at using these and similar conditions to keep us from the practice of hope.

We are not always as closely in touch with ourselves—that is, with our feelings, drives and attitudes—as we think we are or as we need to be. Maybe you find yourself wanting to dismiss what I have been saying about Christian hope in God as so much facile blather. This could be because I referred to weaknesses and vulnerabilities that you have an investment in denying to be true of you. If that is so, I guarantee that you know far less of the joy of hope than you might know and than, quite frankly, I want you to know. I beg you to check up on yourself at this point. How? Well, over and above some honest reflection, I urge you to listen to a voice from the past. Get hold of John Bunyan's *Pilgrim's Progress* (full text); it is a classic pastoral allegory that has been continuously in print for more than three centuries. It fulfills the role of an index to Puritan wisdom on the spiritual life, and in the second half of its second part it has much to say about Mr. Despondency and his daughter Much-afraid, who were rescued from the grip of Giant Despair, about Mr. Feeble-mind and his uncle Mr. Fearing, who made heavier weather of their pilgrimage than did others, and about Mr. Ready-to-halt, who could not go forward at all without crutches. Read the whole book, both parts, then focus on what is said of these characters and how they were ministered to, and I think you will find yourself helped to hope. Meantime, may I tell you some things I had to learn to tell myself in the days when I was a cynic in the making, not doubting the biblical faith but very much disliking both hymns about heaven and the enthusiastic way people sang them.

First, the heart of the Christian hope, both here and hereafter, is the saved sinner's loving fellowship with the Father, the Son and the Holy Spirit, worshiping, obeying and using enterprise to please the divine Three by your service. That is the essential and eternal reality of spiritual life; that is what heaven is fundamentally about; and if I am a real Christian, that is what my present life is beginning to be about already. Here and now, spiritual life brings joy, along with a sense of peace and fulfillment that comes from no other source, and the prospect is that it will continue so forever. This means that every moment in heaven it will be true to say, with Robert Browning, "the best is yet to be," just as each believer may truly say that every moment on earth. It would be sinfully silly to be contemptuous of or offended by so wonderful a prospect.

Second, our benighted, materialist, post-Christian world is actually parading its sinful silliness when it mocks the hope of heaven, and it would be sinfully silly for a Christian to go with the world at this point. Some sentences that C. S. Lewis wrote, and I read, more than half a century ago are worth quoting here:

> Hope is one of the theological virtues. This means that a continual looking forward to the eternal world is not (as some modern people think) a form of escapism or wishful thinking, but one of the things a Christian is meant to do.
>
> There is no need to be worried by facetious people who try to make the Christian hope of "heaven" ridiculous by saying they do not want "to spend eternity playing harps." The answer to such people is that if they cannot understand books written for grown-ups, they should not talk about them. All the scriptural imagery (harps, crowns, gold, etc.) is, of course, a merely symbolical attempt to express the inexpressible. Musical instruments are mentioned because for many people (not all) music is the thing in this present life which most strongly suggests ecstasy and infinity. Crowns are mentioned to suggest the fact that those who are united with God in eternity share his splendor and power and joy. Gold is mentioned to suggest the timelessness of heaven (gold does not rust) and the preciousness of it. People who take these symbols literally might as well think that when Christ told us to be like doves, he meant that we were to lay eggs. (*Mere Christianity* [London: Fontana, 1955], pp. 116, 119)

Third, our gracious God has laid his credit on the line in what he has told us through Christ, through the apostles and through the entire Bible about the life to come, and in the promises about

the future that he has given to all believers (the crutches in Bunyan's allegory without which Mr. Ready-to-halt could not walk).
Those promises have heaven in view constantly. It would be sinfully silly and insulting to God to refuse to believe this teaching
and these promises when we receive other things taught by
Christ, the apostles and the Bible as being divine truth. Can we
ever justify not taking God's word about things? Can we here and
now justify withholding belief from God's own premises about
the future? No, of course we can't. The arrogance of not believing
what God had clearly declared was the sin of Eden; such disbelief
was unwarrantable then and would be equally unwarrantable
now.

An observed effect of depression is loss of power to believe
that any good awaits you, and one of the causes of depression is
feeling you are a misfit or an outsider or a failure. Spiritual depression occurs when such feelings eat away your confidence in
the vast, unmeasured, boundless, free love of your God. I suspect
that you know something of these feelings; many Western Christians, perhaps even most, go through life in a state of undiag-
nosed spiritual depression because these feelings regularly get on
top of them. But the final answer to all feelings of inferiority is to
remind yourself that your God loves, redeems, pardons, restores,
protects, keeps and uses misfits, outsiders and failures no less
than he does beautiful people of the kind that keep crossing your
path and of whom you have been wishing you were one. You will
see this in the Bible studies that follow, which Carolyn and I offer
to God and to you, praying that God may use them to turn many
into the happy hopers that all Christians are called to be.

1

HOPE WHEN MY STRENGTH BRINGS WEAKNESS WITH IT

Samson

JUDGES 14 — 16

N O ONE, SURELY, CAN READ THE SAMSON STORY WITHOUT thinking, *This is tragedy.* Tragedy is a waste of good, a squandering of potential, and Judges 14—16 is a tragic story of much good being wasted because of the way Samson allowed himself to play the fool.

Yet Samson is a hero of faith. We know that because in the eleventh chapter of Hebrews he is named specifically: "And what more shall I say? I do not have time to tell about Gideon, Barak, Samson, Jephthah, David, Samuel, and the prophets" (Heb 11:32). The writer of Hebrews goes on to say that these were men who "through faith conquered kingdoms, administered justice, and gained what was promised; who shut the mouth of lions, quenched the fury of the flames, and escaped the edge of the sword; whose weakness was turned to strength; and who became powerful in battle and routed foreign armies" (vv. 33–34). "Whose weakness was turned to strength"—*strength*, that is, for service that would not otherwise have been rendered. That is part of the story of Samson—as it is part of the story of many more of God's imperfect people.

So Samson was a hero of faith. In fact, a central theme of Samson's story is that God had appointed him to serve as a savior. When the angel of the Lord announced Samson's coming birth to his mother, the angel said that her son would be "set apart to God from birth," and that "he will begin the deliverance of Israel from the hands of the Philistines" (Judg 13:6). So he did. We read that he led and ruled Israel as its judge for twenty years, and it is clear that his actions weakened Philistine control of God's people.

The story of Samson's life as the writer of Judges narrates it is, however, very much like the sort of thing you read in paperback thrillers: women and fights all the way. Samson was undoubtedly a Rambo-type of person, but he is not entirely to blame for that. The book of Judges tells us of a people who lived in a permissive society, and a culture of permissiveness leads naturally to random and irresponsible behavior. We today know that firsthand. "Permissive society" is a description that applies very directly to modern North America. We Westerners live in post-Christian days, and as in Samson's time, the old rules are not regarded. Everyone does what is right in his or her own eyes (see Judg 17:6; 21:25). All kinds of wild things done today involve all kinds of waste of good. We must realize that we live in an era and in a place that is a likely backdrop for just the sort of tragedy that we see in the life of Samson, and take warning.

The essence of tragedy, as I said, is waste of good, the nullifying of potential. And waste is a description of Samson's life, as surveyed here. Samson was a strange sort of hero, as wayward and incorrigible as any juvenile delinquent. He was given enormous physical prowess to battle the Philistines, and he battled them successfully. Scripture says that the Spirit of the Lord came on him in power again and again (Judg 13:25; 14:6, 19; 15:14). And right at the end of his life Samson prayed for and was given strength to bring down the temple of Dagon. He died with the Philistines—as he had prayed that he might. The narrator comments at that point that Samson killed many more when he died than while he lived (16:30). His subduing power over the Philistines is the golden thread that runs through the murky elements of Samson's story. Alongside these escapades Samson, as we noted, was Israel's acknowledged leader for twenty years. We can only guess what he might have achieved had his weaknesses not been what they were.

Flawed Sexuality

For our own warning I must now be specific about the flaws that I see in Samson's character.

First of all, Samson couldn't resist a girl. As a young man he told his parents, much to their distress, "There's a Philistine lass I want to marry." He wooed this pagan woman right at the start of his career, and he ended up with another pagan woman named Delilah. Between the two, Scripture tells of his visit to a prostitute in Gaza. Neither marrying pagans nor bedding prostitutes can please God, but clearly when Samson's sex drive was stirred, nothing could stop him. Nor is this difficult for us to understand. Powerful and successful males still think of physical sexual pleasure as a recreation to which their achievements somehow give them a right, and they still act as if restraints and restrictions that apply to others do not apply

to them. Examples need not be given, though they are bound
to come to mind. Experience has taught us all that this is true.

Flawed Humor

Then too Samson couldn't resist a joke. He was, among other
things, a buffoon who prided himself on being a comic, gaining
admiration and respect by making people laugh at his whimsy
and his wit. I have known people like that, and I expect you have
too. His riddle is a case in point. He wrecked his own wedding
breakfast by setting before the young Philistine men (his wedding guests) the following conundrum:

> Out of the eater, something to eat;
> Out of the strong, something sweet.

"What am I talking about?" he asked. The answer was, as we
know, that Samson remembered the time when he'd found bees
nesting and making honey in the corpse of a lion that he'd killed.
Naturally, he did not expect that anyone would know this. The
young men (not willing to be embarrassed by this outsider, especially when they had each bet a set of clothes that they could
solve any riddle he set before them) put pressure on his bride to
ask him for the correct solution. She did as they requested, then
she told the young men, who at once gave Samson the answer.
Realizing what they had done, Samson then got mad, wrecked
the marriage feast and went home in a fury.

Why did he get mad? Well, because no one was expected to
top Samson's own jokes. His riddle had been solved, he'd been
upstaged by these Philistines, and he didn't like it. His vanity as a
buffoon was hurt, so his euphoria gave way to fury. Unsuccessful
with that joke, Samson soon followed it up with more destructive
humor involving animals, fire and fields of standing grain. He

caught three hundred foxes (how, I wonder?), tied them together by the tail in pairs, fastened a lighted torch to each pair of tails, let the terrified creatures loose and so burned up the entire Philistine harvest. I imagine that as the foxes ran, Samson stood at the edge of the field, laughing his head off. As anyone else might have foreseen, the joke sequence then escalated with unnecessary (and tragic) loss of life (Judg 15:3–17).

On another occasion, after his time with the Gaza prostitute and aware no doubt that an attempt might be made to stop him from leaving, Samson thought it frightfully funny to get up in the middle of the night, wrestle the pair of city gates and gateposts out of the ground, carry them on his back thirty miles, and plant the whole structure on a smooth, rounded hilltop facing Mount Hebron, nowhere near any human habitation. This again is Samson letting his sense of humor lead him into fantastic behavior.

In the end we find Samson teasing his good-time girl Delilah with silly tales about what made him strong. She was plotting his downfall while he was making fun of her. When he finally told her his secret (that as a Nazirite, his hair had never been cut), his joking had fatal results—this time to himself (Judg 16:4–30).

Samson's unbridled humor made him behave repeatedly as a childish buffoon, thoughtless and irresponsible, and this was a real weakness of character. Humor, as such, is a God-given sweetener of life and safeguard of sanity, but we have to control our sense of humor, not let it control us.

Flawed Anger

Samson also had trouble, as we have seen, controlling his temper. Anger is an urge to strike out, hurt and destroy, and Samson's story shows him to be a constantly angry man. He couldn't endure a putdown. One of his fixed ideas, it seems, was that he had to pay people back. Tit for tat was the rule of Samson's life. He would deal with others the way they dealt with him, only worse, so that he got a triumphant revenge and ended up top dog. This attitude appears in his very last prayer: "O God, please strengthen me just once more, and let me with one blow get revenge on the Philistines for my two eyes" (Judg 16:28). Samson did not see that there is more to life than keeping even with the wrongs that are done to us. It was a further character weakness on Samson's part not to be able to control his temper but instead to let anger and pride overflow again and again in hurting other people. (Neighbor love as taught by Jesus and the apostles does the exact opposite: see Mt 5:38–48; Lk 10:25–37; Rom 12:17–21; 1 Jn 3:11–24; 4:7–21.)

In light of that, look again at Samson's practical jokes. People still think that by making others laugh they're somehow vindicating themselves as members of society, so that if their jokes have been expressing malice and anger, that will be forgiven and forgotten because they have given people some fun. Samson was evidently a man of that kind. As we see, his comic actions really have a rather nasty side to them. They are cruel and heartless jokes. They are jokes that express a desire to be one up and to score over the people on whom the jokes are played. Such jokes are not expressions of goodwill. They are funny, but the fun is ugly fun. The jokes are anger in thin disguise. It was a defect in Samson that his conscience seems not to have troubled him about this.

I criticize Samson's jokes with some hesitation because when I started preaching, I was super-serious. The senior minister with whom I was working said to me one day, "Look, you are too serious when you preach for anyone to take you seriously. God gave you humor. Use it!" (He was actually an Irishman, so he said *yummer* [rhymes with *plumber*]). I've been planting jokes in my sermons ever since, and I rather think it is a good idea. But I try to keep them from being malicious or demeaning. I see Samson as a man in the grip of his sense of humor, a man who habitually acted the fool and thought the very fact that he was doing something funny justified his bad behavior.

God's Person

Yet God appointed Samson to be his special servant. Every once in a while in the Samson story up pops a reminder of the fact that Samson is God's man, set apart for God's work, and it is God who is overruling the course of Samson's actions and experience. It is this part of the Samson story that brings us hope. We too live tragic-comic flawed lives, lives full of mistakes and deficiencies, lives in which what we think of as our strengths take us ego-hopping and so become our real weakness. But God was God to Samson—and is God to us.

Oddly, there are things in the Samson story that remind us of the Lord Jesus—another person miraculously born for the purposes of God's kingdom. Jesus had a sense of humor also. True, it was a rather grim and sharp sense of humor. But we are surely meant to smile a bit at the thought of a camel going through the eye of a needle or a man with a plank sticking out of his own eye trying to get a speck out of someone else's eye. Yet Jesus wasn't enslaved to his humor. He was man of courtesy, wisdom, goodwill and restraint in a way that Samson never was.

As for self-control, not losing one's temper, Jesus was reviled but did not revile again. He committed himself to the one who judges justly. That's true human maturity, a maturity that all we who are Christ's are called to aim at (see 1 Pet 2:19–23). In this respect Jesus and Samson are polar opposites.

Christian Caution

The story of Samson is a cautionary tale, and it is appropriate that we Christians take Samson's biography as a warning to ourselves. Samson was physically strong, that's true. At the moments when God's Spirit fell on him, God gave him unbelievable strength. But this very strength brought weakness—the specific weaknesses of self-centeredness, self-reliance, self-indulgence and self-satisfaction. All four are clearly here in Samson's track record. Had he been less spectacularly strong, he would have been less vulnerable to these attitudes. As it was, he fought the Philistines well but seems to have made no progress at all in the war with sin—which meant that all through his life he was weak within.

We evangelical Christians are strong too in at least one sense, that is, numerically. When statisticians count numbers, they tell us that there are about forty million of us in the United States alone. We have seminaries, technologies and the megachurch movement. The ministry and impact of a giant-sized Southern Baptist leader named Billy Graham, honorary chaplain to North America, has been incalculable, and he is, as we say, "one of us." Our literature ministry expands and expands. God has given Christians impressive strength, yet our very strength makes us vulnerable. Are we in danger of falling victim to some of the same self-destructive weaknesses we see in Samson? That, I think, is a question we must face very seriously.

Evangelical Christians live in an enclave. It is a large enclave, but it is an enclave all the same. We cannot escape our family relationship to each other. Who and what we are individually impacts all of us. And things in our enclave are not always what they should be. We need purity of heart—especially in sexual matters. We know that there are folk in our Christian circles today whose sexual lives are all too similar to Samson's. Beyond sexual purity there was a certain high quality of character that Samson never attained, and in evangelical circles we don't always attain that quality either. In some of our Christian ministries we see an unwillingness to accept accountability, a desire to lead others and to be our own boss as we do so. We see emotional attitudes—resentment, bad temper, vindictiveness, discourtesy, unlove—that spell the same lack of maturity and sanctity that Samson displayed. Christians are quarrelsome. Christians are conceited. Christians are power-hungry egoists; we build empires. This happens over and over again.

These character flaws (Samson's and ours) are real weaknesses—weaknesses that can have a tragic effect both on our personal lives and on the impact that our evangelical strength makes in North America today. Defects of character destroy credibility in no time. In my travels I have spoken many times on the character of Samson. Every time I speak of him, I see in him a disturbing mirror of what I actually observe around me. So now I shall offer some lessons from Samson, this man of flawed character, divine vocation and real if unsteady faith.

On Being Weak and Being Strong

Where we feel strong, there we may very easily be weak. The Scriptures say, "If you think you are standing firm, be careful that you don't fall!" (1 Cor 10:12). Let everyone who loves to be independent in Christ realize the danger of being independent of Christ. Samson was a loner; he did his own thinking. But that wasn't the path of blessing from every standpoint. Had he listened more to his parents (note Judg 14:2-4) and had he made himself accountable to elders and friends (note 15:7-13), he would surely have done better and honored God more. So mistrust your own sense of strength and realize your own need for fellowship and accountability. We all need that to keep us in order.

And realize that God in his mercy may have to deal with us eventually as he dealt with Samson. Through Delilah's treachery Samson was taken captive by the Philistines. He was blinded; they cut off his hair; the strength God had given him seemed gone forever; his usefulness seemed to have gone as well. In the goodness of God Samson recovered just enough strength for the final act of his life. We cannot help thinking, however, how much better it would have been if Samson had never got involved with Delilah in the first place.

But there's a message here for us. God may have to weaken us and bring us down at the points where we thought we were strong in order that we may become truly strong in real dependence on himself. He's done that before, and he may have to do it again—perhaps on a grand scale with Christians in North America, maybe on a personal level with you and me. If he does, there will be mercy in it. It will be God working to make some sense out of rambling lives that have reached the point where it seems that nothing good can come from them anymore.

One more encouraging thought from Samson's story. God does use us. He uses us right now in spite of our flaws. He is a kindly God and uses flawed people as a part of his regular agenda. No matter how conscious we are of our own limitations, shortcomings and sins, we may look to God to make use of us again—and in his great mercy he will.

Christians live by faith in Jesus Christ, which means we live by being forgiven. And Christians (forgiven sinners) are given a share in God's work in a way that, over and over, goes beyond anything we could have expected—certainly anything that we deserve. Samson's story is not all gloom and doom and despair. It shows that we serve a gracious God who could and did use even a wild man such as Samson was. So in spite of all our shortcomings there is hope that God will reveal a positive role for you and me in the affairs of his kingdom.

So let us take courage and learn from Samson's story the lessons it has for us. We must seek to get our lives—and keep our lives—in a shape that will glorify God. That's not easy. It means fighting our sins, disciplining our thoughts, changing our attitudes and critiquing our desires in a way that Samson did not try to do. But let's trust in the Lord who uses flawed human material for his glory, and by faith let's seek strength to serve God in good works and good attitudes that at this moment we feel are beyond us. Those who seek find; for Samson's God, who is our God, is a God of great patience and great grace. Thus there is great hope for us all. Praise his name.

Holy Father, you know us, you have loved us and redeemed us through the blood-shedding of your Son, and exalted us to the glorious dignity of being your children and heirs. Keep us mindful of our privileged identity, and teach us to live lives that are Christlike in their maturity of faith and hope, their consistency in aiming to please you, and their humility in looking to you for the help we need at all times. Make us honest in recognizing our weaknesses of character and conduct, and in repenting of our sins. Lead us not into temptation but deliver us from evil. So may we follow your servant Samson in contending for the welfare of your people, and by your grace go beyond him in self-denial and purity of heart and life. Through Jesus Christ, our Savior and our Lord. Amen.

Study

1. Read the biblical account of Samson's life in Judges 14—16.

2. What evidences do you see of God's kindness in this description of Samson's life?

3. Review the ways that Samson used his enormous physical strength. What character weaknesses do these actions suggest?

4. What are some of your own areas of strength?

5. What cautions can you take so that your strength does not become a source of weakness?

6. What situations tempt you to use humor as a weapon?

7. Before Samson was born an angel spoke to his mother about her son (see Judg 13:3–5). How might the angel's words at that time have helped Samson's mother as she witnessed the events in his life?

8. Hebrews 11:32–34 speaks of Samson as one whose "weakness was turned to strength." In what ways did God use Samson—in spite of his flaws?

9. One of Samson's weaknesses was the way he misused his strength. What misuses of power seem especially tempting to Christians?

10. As you consider some of your own flaws, what warnings and what encouragement do you take from the Samson story?

Pray

■ Spend several moments in quiet contemplation asking God to remind you of some of the strengths that he has given you. List several of these as a reminder of his kindness to you and of the responsibilities he has given you to use those strengths for his glory.

■ Even though it may be painful, ask God to reveal some of the flaws in your character. (It may be appropriate to kneel for this prayer communication.) One by one in prayer, turn these flaws over to God, asking his forgiveness. Ask also for his strength as you attempt to overcome your flaws.

■ Sometimes we can best overcome our weaknesses when we join with one or two others who will pray for us and regularly ask us how we are doing in these weak areas. Consider, in prayer, whether this may be true for you. If it seems appropriate, begin a search for partners in accountability.

■ God uses us "right now" in spite of our flaws. Thank God for this. Ask that he will point out to you this day how you can serve him.

Write

Prayerfully review the section in this chapter titled "On Being Weak and Being Strong" (pp. 33-35). Ask God to show you how it ought to impact who you are and what you do. Jot notes on your impressions. Then write a prayer of response to God.

2

HOPE WHEN I BELONG TO AN UNHAPPY FAMILY

Jacob

GENESIS 25; 27—49

I HAVE TWO REASONS FOR PUTTING JACOB UNDER THE MICRO-
scope, over and above the fact that he is my namesake. (*Jacobus*
is Greek for Jacob, and *James* is English for Jacobus.) The first
reason is that he is a fascinating mixture. He had a heart both for
gain and for God, and this two-sidedness led to the crisis of his
life—as we shall see. When Jacob was born, he was one of twins,
and he came out of his mother's womb with his hand holding on
to his brother's heel. His name memorialized that: *Jacob* means
"the one who grasps the heel," with the implication of pulling
someone else down in order to get ahead.

As we go through the story of Jacob the adult, we shall find
that in many ways he lived up to his name. He was something of
a grabber, an exploiter, a manipulator and a cheat. Not that the
grabbing and the exploiting and the manipulating and the cheat-
ing, as we shall see, brought Jacob happiness any more than it

brought happiness to the people who were his victims; instead, it brought tension and strain and ill will—a warning for us. Only when his passion for gain was finally put second to his passion for God did his life settle down. That was after Jacob tried for many years to be both worldly and godly, both on the make and under the mercy, a course of action that led to the crisis at Jabbok—which, as we shall see, was the turning point of his whole existence.

There is a second reason why I write about Jacob. The story of Jacob is part of the story of a family. Jacob was both the product and inevitably therefore the producer of what we nowadays call a dysfunctional family, which is regularly a generation-to-generation business. The defects in your upbringing, in your family of origin, get passed on by you to the family that you raise. That's what happened in Jacob's family, and it happens now. We ask, what is the book of Genesis about? Different answers are given. A common—and correct—answer is that Genesis is the book of beginnings, the book in which we see the beginning of the world, of human history and of God's plan of grace.

But there's another way of looking at the book, less common but equally correct. From chapter 12 to chapter 50 Genesis is about a dysfunctional family: Abraham's family, traced through three generations, down to the death of Jacob. What you see in the story, looked at from that standpoint, is God's grace to this one flawed family, God's grace dealing with the dysfunctional relations of these dysfunctional people. And God's grace triumphs in the end in the lives of Abraham and Isaac and Jacob, and of Joseph and his brothers as well. By seeing God's grace to Jacob's family, in spite of all the pain its members inflicted on each other, we can find hope for our own. One of the things you see most gloriously in this family story is the many-sidedness of the grace that

God shows: the grace that forgives and the grace that forbears, the grace that helps and the grace that holds, the grace that renews and the grace that restores, as members of the family fumble and stumble and make mistakes and relationships go wrong. Our God is a God of great grace. If you feel as many nowadays do that you are a victim of dysfunctional or broken family relationships, there is much to encourage and help you in the story of Jacob.

Jacob's story begins in the twenty-fifth chapter of Genesis, right in the middle of the larger family narrative. Jacob appears in that story as to some extent a victim of a family pattern and to some extent a victimizer himself, imposing the same bad family pattern on others. This was, of course, a special family: God was working with this family because it was central to his purpose of redemption for the world. That purpose reached its climax in the life and death and rising and ascension and heavenly reign of the Lord Jesus, the incarnate Son of God who in his humanity descends from Abraham and Isaac and Jacob. We who know the Lord Jesus are to live in his name, that is, as his representatives and agents, confident that he himself is with us by his Spirit. We must never forget then that Christ is with us now to forgive and to restore and to strengthen and to counsel and so to help us not to make the mistakes that were made centuries before in the days of the patriarchs.

The story of this dysfunctional family began with God's selecting Abraham and saying, "I will make of you a great nation and in you and through you all families of the earth will be blessed" (see Gen 12:2-3). We are inheritors of that blessing through Jesus Christ our Savior, and it is in the presence of Christ with the power of Christ at hand to help us that we move into the present study. If perchance things that I write become painful because they remind you of dysfunction in your own family, remember that our Savior forbears and forgives and restores. And Christians are always and only disciples of Jesus Christ, who live day by day through being forgiven and who couldn't live a single day without being forgiven. That New Testament perspective must be basic for us as we dig into the early history of the family from which Jesus eventually came.

Jacob's Family Tree

First we will look at some of the background of Jacob's family, and then we are going to follow his course up to and beyond the watershed event recorded in Genesis 32. There's a sort of motto, a somber dictum, which it seems to me has to be written over the whole of Jacob's story up to that point: *Adversarial affection produces adversarial ambition.* Adversarial affection means, in practice, favoritism. When, as was the case with Jacob, a mother brings up one of her children as a favorite who's made to feel that Mom loves me more than she loves any of my siblings, that adversarial affection on the part of the parent gets internalized and when the child becomes an adult, he or she still retains the feeling of being better than others. "Mother always thought so. I take her word for it. So my aim in life is always going to be to get ahead, to outsmart everyone else, to do them down. I'm going to make it and never mind who gets hurt in the process."

This was Jacob's heritage, alas, from his mother, Rebekah. Esau, Jacob's twin, was Isaac's favorite, but Rebekah, it seems, was a much more forceful person than Isaac, as well as being a good deal younger, and it was her favoritism that shaped Jacob. What we see therefore in Jacob's story right up to the beginning of chapter 32 is Jacob living out the idea that he was always meant to be number one and acting as if he had some kind of right (or as we say nowadays, "entitlement") to exploit and manipulate and walk over other people in the process. That was what God changed permanently at Peniel, as we shall see.

Jacob grows up, then, on the one hand ambitious and on the other hand what I call a corner-cutter. He's an eager beaver. You could call him an entrepreneur and a businessman. Getting ahead is his consistent goal. So first he persuades Esau, his elder twin brother (elder by minutes), to sell him his birthright. Esau comes in famished and says, "Give me some of that fine food you've got there." And Jacob says, "All right, if you'll give me your birthright." Esau is just hungry, and he isn't thinking, so he says, "What's my birthright to me? You can have it, but give me some of that good grub." So the deal is done. Here is Jacob beginning to exploit the family situation in order to gain what wasn't his by right (see Gen 25:24–34).

Jacob's Alienation

Jacob also stole Esau's blessing. That was something his mother, I'm sorry to say, put him up to (see Gen 27). Isaac had said, "Esau, you're my elder son, so go out and shoot some game and make a stew. I love stew. And in the joy of the good food, I will give you my blessing." Then Rebekah said to Jacob, "We'll outsmart Esau on this one." She cooked a stew. Jacob at her suggestion disguised himself with hair on his hands so he would feel like Esau when Isaac touched him—and he got Esau's blessing. So when Esau came in, the blessing of the firstborn had already been given to Jacob, and as things were understood in those days, it could not be adjusted or recalled. You can't wonder that Esau said, "This is too much! I'd like to kill that brother of mine. In due course, I will." And Rebekah said to Jacob, "You'd better leave, or else."

It's obvious that Rebekah and Isaac weren't close at this time.

Rebekah now went to Isaac and said, "I think it would be a good idea to send Jacob to Laban to make sure that he marries in the family and doesn't marry a pagan woman like Esau did." Evidently Jacob had learned the art of manipulation from his mother. Oh yes, she rightly wanted the best for Jacob, but it was not good that she had this adversarial attitude toward Esau, his father's favorite. It shouldn't be like that in families! But it was like that in this family, and so Rebekah devised this way of getting Jacob off the premises with his father's blessing so that Esau in his fury would not be able to follow through on his murderous threat.

So off went Jacob, who spent, as it turned out, twenty years with Laban. First he worked for seven years in order to earn Rachel, the younger daughter he loved, as his bride. Now here the biter was bit—Laban also was an exploiter. Laban too was not above dirty tricks. Later there were battles of wits in which Jacob got the better of Laban (see Gen 30:25—31:55), but at this point he was made a fool of. When the wedding day came, Laban married Leah, the elder daughter, to Jacob. The bride was fully veiled at the wedding ceremony, so Jacob was effectively bamboozled. Then when the deed was done, Laban said blandly to Jacob, "Oh, well, we always marry the older daughter first. Didn't you know? And for seven more years' work you can have Rachel as well."

So Jacob put in seven more years, and then he did wed Rachel, and so was in a state of what we call polygamy, which means having more than one wife. Some people think this would be wonderful, but in fact polygamy has always been miserable because of jealousy between the wives—and both of them, or however many there are, then take it out on the husband. It's all there in Jacob's story. The result of Jacob's having two wives plus later the handmaid of each of them, which makes four (although according to the ancient convention the handmaid's children would count as her mistress's children and so make up for the mistress's inability to conceive), was certainly not domestic happiness. Jacob produced a sizable family, but he did not have much joy otherwise—although he grew very rich over the years. Then at last he decided the best course would be to go home. That's the story of Jacob's heart for gain and what came of it.

Jacob and God

But there's more to the story than this. The other side of Jacob's character, right from the time we meet him, is that with his heart for gain he also had a heart for God, given him by God himself—God who always takes the initiative in grace. God wanted Jacob as his man, and Jacob wanted God as his God. When Jacob had left home to go to Laban, he was granted a vision—a ladder up to heaven. God stood at the top of the ladder and spoke words of love to Jacob, and Jacob committed himself to God (see Gen 28:10-22). Thank God when the members of our families want God. It's a sad thing when they don't. Then all we can do is pray that God will stir in their hearts a desire for himself. But Jacob, son and heir in Isaac's family, had that desire all along, as it seems—and pledged himself to God accordingly (see Gen 28:10–22).

Now when Jacob wanted to go home, he was not foolish enough to leave Laban before he had a word from God to assure him that it was the right thing to do. Jacob did not make the mistake that so many make of saying in effect to God, "This is what I want to do, so Lord, I'm asking you to bless it." To do that is the opposite of reverence. It says that I have made up my own mind about what I intend to do, and I'm now trying to manipulate God to fit him in with my plans. We can never do that! And Jacob did not try to do it. In Genesis 30:25 we find him saying to Laban, "Send me on my way so that I can go back to my own homeland." But it was much later when, as Genesis 31:3 records, the Lord said, "Go back to the land of your fathers and to your relatives, *and I will be with you*" [emphasis mine]. That's a key phrase, implying God's fellowship, protection and enrichment all in one. It was a vital promise to Jacob, several times repeated as God guided Jacob in his travels. (To verify that look at Gen 28:15; 31:3–5; 35:3; 46:4.) Let us be clear on this: It's not for us to make any significant move until we've gone to the throne of God and sought his assurance that he will be with us, and we may have to wait some time before that assurance comes.

So God has given the word some six years after Jacob married Rachel, and now at last Jacob is on the way. He takes with him, in the manner of a traveling sheik, all his cattle, goats and sheep. He's become a rich man, and it is quite a substantial caravan that he and his staff lead across country.

The Long Way Home

What happens? Genesis 32 tells us that Jacob sends ahead of him a message to Esau, his brother, with whom he hasn't communicated since he stole Esau's blessing. Though it's been twenty years he's afraid that Esau is still cherishing murder in his heart, so when he hears from his messenger that Esau is coming to meet him with four hundred armed men, he panics. "Jacob, eh," he could hear Esau saying, "I'll see that he doesn't get away this time." And now we are at the turning point of Jacob's life.

Genesis 32:9–12 tells us that Jacob prayed. He invokes God's faithfulness thus far and makes this the basis for his plea that God will continue to watch over him—because God is his only hope. Jacob knows that. This is perhaps the most desperate prayer he's ever made. It deserves detailed study, which we cannot give it here. Then night falls and Jacob breaks up the gift he has planned. He splits his own flocks and herds, from which he has already taken a large gift for Esau, and he sends them ahead separately. He wants to make these flocks and their shepherds into a series of distinct signs of the wealth he brings and from which he may well in the future give Esau more. He hopes all of this will mollify Esau before Esau meets him. Also, as a realist he is providing for the worst case: if Esau attacks one group, the rest, being separate, may escape (v. 8). Then he sees his wives and their maidservants and his eleven sons across the ford of the Jabbok, a brook that feeds into the Jordan, and sends them on ahead. Now he is left alone.

Why does he stay behind? Clearly because he's in a blue funk, and he can't bring himself to resume traveling to meet Esau. Memories of how long ago he heartlessly took advantage of Esau and fears of Esau's continuing fury and purpose of revenge flood his heart. Now he has to face the consequences of his guilty, shameful go-getting; understandably he's crumpling under the strain. He knows God is his only hope, and he's got to pray again. Perhaps he begins.

What comes next is Jacob's own story. It couldn't be anyone else's story, because no human observer was there. This is what Jacob told his family afterward: "A man wrestled with me till daybreak." What are we to make of it? Jacob could not say where the man came from. He only knew that as his mind was in turmoil and he was trying to focus on God, someone engaged him in hand-to-hand combat. Afterward Jacob called the place Peniel, which means "face of God," for he realized that this had been what we call a theophany, a manifestation of God to him: "I saw God face to face."

God as Wrestler

The divine visitor, unrecognized as yet, leaped upon Jacob, and they wrestled through the night. In wrestling the aim is to get the other fellow down and keep him down, and clearly that's what Jacob thought and felt that the visitor was trying to do to him. What do we make of that? The theophany principle is that God always appears to people in the form in which it will most help them to meet him—as an indestructible burning bush to Moses, as a soldier to Joshua, as an enthroned monarch to Isaiah and Ezekiel; and here God appears as a wrestler, forcing Jacob to the ground.

What this wrestling match shows us is that God has to bring us down before he can raise us up. Down from what? Down from the way that we set ourselves up in pride and self-sufficiency and cleverness and initiative and self-reliance and conscious adversarial tactics so that we can outsmart other people. This had been Jacob's way, and now all his self-serving habits were being squeezed out of him. That's what God was doing as he wrestled with Jacob. Rebekah's spoiled boy certainly needed this treatment and needed it badly, but let us be clear that original sin, the deepest root of pride and self-serving, is a universal disease, and we all need the same treatment to some extent.

Jacob felt at first that here was an enemy. Then he thought, *Enemy or not, I can hold my own with him. At least I can wrestle.* And in his not-yet-quite-demolished self-sufficiency, at first he thought he could win. Then the person with whom he was wrestling touched his hip. In a moment the hip was out of joint—and Jacob was lame. He could keep struggling, but now he had no hope of winning the contest. Did Jacob have a sense of being overcome, a sense of total and permanent weakness that would be with him for the rest of his life? My guess is that he did. Did he realize that this was precisely what God was aiming at? How long it took him to realize this we do not know. But we, reading the story—in light of all that we know from the rest of the Bible about God's ways—can see it clearly: our God is a God who blesses us through breaking us, and he was blessing Jacob by making him permanently lame.

I imagine that Jacob limped and needed a staff to walk with every day from then on. But God, having brought him down in this drastic way, now has an unexpected and momentous word of encouragement for him. "Your name will . . . be . . . Israel [meaning, *he struggles with God*], because you have struggled with God and with men and have overcome" (Gen 32:28). What had felt like the end of his ego was really the beginning of his true blessing. What had felt like final defeat in life's battle was actually the only kind of victory that matters—the dawning of the real self-despair that precedes the blossoming of real Hebrews-11-type faith. With good reason "Jacob called the place Peniel, saying, 'It is because I saw God face to face, and yet my life was spared'" (v. 30). If we follow the story further, we shall find that more unexpected blessings are waiting for Jacob, starting with the fact that when he and Esau meet, Esau is delighted to see him.

Broken by God's Love

As a commentary on this story of Jacob being broken so that he might be blessed, let me tell you of a Regent College alumnus who was called to missionary service in Africa. There he had a horrific motor accident, which has left him lame for life. Back in Vancouver he told the story in chapel. Twice lying in the hospital, hardly able to gather his thoughts, he had gotten to the point of asking, "Lord, why have you done this? Why has this happened to me?" Then he said, "There came back to me a phrase from Deuteronomy over and over, 'Because I love you, because I love you, because I love you.' " That was why God lamed Jacob, and that is why again and again grisly things happen to you and me. In God's gracious dealing with us he breaks us and humbles us and brings us down lower than we ever thought it was possible for people to go. What feels like death is then followed by what we find to be resurrection. It happens in Christian lives repeatedly. As the last line of a poem written by John Donne on his deathbed put it: "Therefore, that he may raise, the Lord throws down."

Jacob at Home

But Jacob's experience of family trouble did not end with his reconciliation with Esau. The shortcomings and pains of one generation often filter through to the next, and so it was in this case. Jacob had a heart for his family and loved his children. But like Rebekah, who had brought him up on the principle of favoritism, spoiling him by making him her favorite son, when Jacob had children, he had favorites too. And the trouble that later hit his family stemmed directly from this favoritism. I suspect that Jacob never saw it. Things that shape us in our earliest youth may be very disorderly and very sinful, but we find it hard to see this or even to be aware of these things—because they have always been part of us. The idea that favoritism was natural and acceptable, even right and proper, in a family was part of Jacob's mindset. It doesn't look as if he ever got over it.

Observe what harm that particular failing brought. Jacob showed favoritism first of all regarding his wives. He loved Rachel a lot more than he loved Leah, and he let it show. That led to bitterness at home from the start. Favoritism always arouses fury in the people who are made to feel that they are not the favorite, but someone else is. And from that fury comes folly. Nonfavorite children will behave in a wild way; they're trying to work their mad off. They're angry with their parents for the favoritism, they're angry with their brother or sister for being the favorite, and they take their anger out on other people. Our world is full of people who have suffered in this way and are now irascible, hostile adults. They are taking their childhood hurts out on whoever is handy for the purpose. We know them, and perhaps to some extent we are them. Watching what happened in Jacob's family will help us understand such people and will point us to the remedy that so many of us actually need.

In Jacob's family, where Benjamin and Joseph, the two youngest, were the favorites, and Jacob's relation to his other offspring was cooler, there was murder: Levi and Simeon killed the males of a whole community—as we see in Genesis 34. There was incest, which involved Reuben (Gen 35:22). There was a nasty business in which Judah unwittingly had sex with his daughter-in-law, thinking she was a prostitute (Gen 38). The fact that this all happened in Jacob's family, I think, says something rather sad about Jacob as a parent.

Then there was the whole affair of Joseph. Joseph was the prime favorite because he was Rachel's boy. All the other sons were made to feel that they were inferior to him. Joseph came to feel that primacy among them was his right. He had dreams that suggested primacy, and he told those dreams to the family and seemed to have been quite surprised when the family didn't appreciate them. His brothers got furious with him. They sold him into Egypt, dipped his ornamental robe in animal's blood, took it back to Jacob and said, "See what we found? Isn't this Joseph's?" Then they stood by quite pokerfaced while Jacob broke his heart over his belief that Joseph, his favorite son, had been killed by a wild animal (Gen 37). What does that tell you about the dynamics of the family?

The Process of Healing

We know what finally happened. When Joseph was in full charge of Egypt's economy, and the famine had Canaan in its grip, Joseph's brothers went down to Egypt to buy grain. Joseph at first played a game with them, a sort of tit-for-tat in light of the way they had sold him years before. But he could not keep the game up for long. Joseph was a godly fellow and soon made himself known to his brothers, and there was a tearful reunion— tearful this time because of joy, not sorrow. Joseph sent them home with wealth and with carts. (Nowadays it would be a convoy of trucks, I suppose. Then it was ox carts.) "You're to bring our father and all your possessions. You're to emigrate down here to Egypt so that you can live on the fat of the land." That's what Joseph told his brothers. So they came back to Jacob and told him that Joseph was still alive and was summoning them to Egypt so that he could be their savior from starvation and share with them the better life that was his (Gen 42—45). Rightly do Bible teachers point to Joseph as a model in many ways of Jesus, the Savior. As you glance at the story you see the parallels.

Jacob's abiding pain at losing Joseph had been augmented by what he thought was the permanent loss of Simeon and Benjamin as well (for Jacob's misery, see Gen 37:34–35; 42:36— 43:14), and the discovery that all the bad news had become good news at first took his breath away. But then, tottery centenarian that he was, he resolved to accept Joseph's gracious magisterial summons and leave for the new land and the new life. So finally we see Jacob doing what, as the father of the family, he should have been doing at all levels all along. Jacob leads his whole family along the path of faithful obedience, where God is with them. In Genesis 46:2–4 we read how in a night vision God spoke to Jacob (here significantly referred to by his God-given name, Israel) and promised to go down to Egypt with him and bless the family there. It is pleasant to imagine old Jacob, with shaking voice and overflowing heart, sharing all this with the whole clan at breakfast the next day. So at last Jacob's children are able to see what it means for God to be with someone: they see it in their dad.

Here is the picture of what we must hope by God's grace to see in every Christian family. Favoritism, if it is ever present, must become a thing of the past, as seemingly became the case in Egypt, and all the children should be finding and sharing with their children the full blessing that their parents knew. God grant that's how it will be in your family. Hope for it; work for it; pray for it; wait for it patiently; and never grow apathetic about it.

Family Sin and Family Grace

Much of Jacob's story carries messages for us today. Jacob, the product of a somewhat dysfunctional marriage, was a spoiled boy, his mother's darling, who early on showed himself ambitious in an adversarial way, as his mother's attitude had taught him to be, and much greedier for gain than was good for him. In this he was like many young and middle-aged people in the modern West, where children are still spoiled and material gain is the only goal that many have. We need to rethink the assumptions on which family nurture is nowadays based.

Because Jacob was an uninhibited, self-centered go-getter, he made enemies. Both Esau and Laban resented his outmaneuvering of them, and who can wonder? Nobody likes being outsmarted, and nobody feels friendly to those who exploit them. Contempt for others (which was what Jacob's maneuvers really involved) regularly comes home to roost. Neighbor love should start with family love. This is surely a word for our time.

Because Jacob had a heart for God as well as for gain, God mercifully guided him, guarded him and changed him for the better. The change process was, however, traumatic and left him permanently lame. Other proud hearts may need comparable treatment today, and God one way or another may give it. It will be an act of grace if and when he does, however low we may be brought in the process.

Because favoritism was so much part of his own upbringing, Jacob had a blind spot here and sowed bitterness among his own sons by his favoritism to Joseph, which had catastrophic results. The generation-to-generation patterns of dysfunction in the family are exceedingly hard to break.

Because God is wonderfully gracious to all who seek him, Jacob was blessed beyond and indeed contrary to anything he deserved. The way in which Joseph finally saved the family from lethal starvation modeled in material terms the saving relationship implicit in God's covenant promise to be "with" Jacob and explicit in the present era through the reconciling ministry and transforming friendship of our Lord Jesus Christ.

Because grace and graciousness generate gratitude and goodwill, it looks as if the kindness and forgiveness that Joseph showed to his brothers defused the spirit of alienation and opened a new chapter of mutual affection among Jacob's sons. Rather than cherishing a vision of himself as a victim, Joseph instead saw himself as one whom God had blessed, and he infected his brothers with the same happy point of view. For Christians in dysfunctional families Joseph is a wonderful model.

Because Jacob, though lamed by divine action, appreciated how good God had been to him, he spoke of it constantly, testifying and adoring, just as those whom Christ has saved should do. We need to take all these things to heart. We serve a God who loves us, and we're to interpret everything that happens to us in terms of the love of God. But if perhaps we feel that we have failed our God and our own families, we must remember that as Christians we live by being forgiven. Our God is endlessly gracious. We must confess our follies and receive his forgiveness and then look to him to help us forward. As there was recovery first for Jacob and then for his family, so there is hope in God for us and ours. So whatever you do, don't give up on either your God or your family—your parents, your children, your siblings or whomever. God has a heart for families, so seek his blessing for yours.

Holy Father, we bow before you in great humility for we are flawed, sinful human beings, and our relationships show it— often in ways of which we're not aware. Many of us still struggle with resentment and self-pity by reason of our memories of inadequate family life and deficient parenting. And many of us carry the responsibility of family life to give nurture and direction in the way of God to a new generation. Our consciences tell us that often we fail to fulfill that responsibility as we should. Have mercy on us, Lord, and as by your grace you have brought us to Christ in whom are hid all the treasures of wisdom and knowledge, and from whom we may draw all the resources that we need, so help us to honor you in our family life. Grant us, we pray, a sensitive conscience about family matters and grant us all the joy of seeing the next generation, the children that you have entrusted to us, coming to share our faith and walk in your way. Hear us, Lord, as thus we pray, and write these things in our hearts for the blessing of others and the glory of your name, for Jesus' sake. Amen.

Study

1. What do you see of yourself in Jacob?

2. Read Genesis 32:1–32. What precautions did Jacob take that might lead to a peaceful meeting with his brother?

3. Study Jacob's prayer in verses 9–12. What do the various phrases of his prayer suggest about his relationship with God?

4. Focus on verses 22–32. In what way was this encounter with God different from the relationship suggested by his prayer?

5. In what ways do you think Jacob would be different because of this encounter with God?

6. If you were to have a wrestling match with God, what would it likely be about?

7. Review the section titled "God as Wrestler" (pp. 48-49). One of the concluding statements there is "our God is a God who blesses us through breaking us." When and how have you found that to be true?

8. God reveals himself in ways most important to the person he meets—as he did to Moses, Joshua, Isaiah and Ezekiel. Most of us have not met God in ways as significant as a theophany, yet he does meet us. How has God revealed himself in a way that was particularly appropriate for you?

9. Jacob limped, probably all of his life, after his encounter with God. In view of what you know of Jacob's life thus far, how was this limp likely to influence the person he was becoming?

10. What long-term impact has God made on you?

11. What could Jacob have learned about God as a result of his trip to Egypt?

12. What lessons from Jacob's life do you want to carry into your own family?

Pray

Divide Jacob's prayer of Genesis 32:9–12 into four parts and use it as an outline for your own praying.

■ "O God of my father Abraham, God of my father Isaac, O LORD, who said to me, 'Go back to your country and your relatives and I will make you prosper.'"

Talk to God about your own past experience with him, particularly as it relates to your family. Bring to him the current work that he has placed in your hand.

■ "I am unworthy of all the kindness and faithfulness you have shown your servant. I had only my staff when I crossed this Jordan, but now I have become two groups."

Give thanks to God for all that he has given you, acknowledging that these did not come by your own efforts alone. Express praise for God's character and your own need and dependence on him.

■ "Save me, I pray, from the hand of my brother Esau, for I am afraid he will come and attack me, and also the mothers with their children."

Bring to God your most serious current problem. Be honest about your fears and any sense of inadequacy. Ask for his intervention to bring about what is right and good.

■ "But you have said, 'I will surely make you prosper and will make your descendants like the sand of the sea, which cannot be counted.' "

Remind God (and yourself) of his promises toward you. God's word to you from Isaiah can serve as a starting point for your prayer: "You are my servant; I have chosen you and have not rejected you. So do not fear, for I am with you; do not be dismayed, for I am your God. I will strengthen you and help you; I will uphold you with my righteous right hand" (Is 41:9–10).

Write

"We serve a God who loves us, and we're to interpret everything that happens to us in terms of the love of God" (p. 55).

Meditate on this sentence as it relates to the events in your own life. As you recall events of joy, satisfaction and pain, write an honest response to God.

3

HOPE WHEN I AM BARELY NOTICED AND NOT TRUSTED

Manoah's Wife

JUDGES 13

L ET ME TELL YOU A STORY YOU MAY NOT HAVE HEARD. IF YOU have, it's good enough to revisit, as I'm sure you will agree.

There was once a man who had a pet gorilla and taught it to play golf. The gorilla made such good progress that soon its owner was challenging the professional at the local golf club to a match. The professional thought that playing golf with a gorilla was ridiculous, but what he said to the gorilla's owner was, "Sure, I'll play your gorilla if we may put some money on it." The golf pro thought it would be easy money for himself, of course. So they staked one hundred dollars each. On the day of the match they went down together to the first tee. The professional golfer gave the gorilla the honor, and the gorilla teed up for his drive. Now it was a long hole, but down the fairway went the ball to lie very nicely placed on the green, four hundred yards away. The professional blinked and said to the gorilla's owner, "I never expected to see a gorilla make a stroke like that. Do you think he could do it again?" "Oh, yes," said the gorilla's owner. "He's very consistent." So the owner whispered into the gorilla's ear, and the gorilla teed up once more and swung his driver. Down the fairway went the second ball to lie alongside the first on the green. The professional golfer broke into a cold sweat and said, "I can't compete with that. I give you the match right now. Here's your money." So they walked back to the clubhouse with the professional going on and on about the two strokes that he'd seen the gorilla make. Eventually he said to the gorilla's owner, "If he's like that off the tee, whatever is he like on the green?" And the gorilla's owner said to him, "Oh, he's very consistent. Every stroke—four hundred yards."

God's Surprises

Now I tell that tale of the four-hundred-yard gorilla not to warn against golf or gorillas or gambling but to remind us all that life is full of surprises. As there are surprises in the punch lines of all the best jokes, so there are periodic surprises in every human life, and specifically so in the lives of God's people. It is God's way to spring surprises—startling surprises in their impact, happy surprises in their outcome—again and again.

Judges 13 tells how he did this to Samson's parents, Manoah and Mrs. Manoah—as we have to call her because we're not told her name. In verses 17–20 we read how Manoah asked the name of a mysterious visitor who had come to their home, and the visitor did not give Manoah an answer—or rather he gave an answer that was quite unclear—something to the effect of, "There is more to me than ever you can understand, and I'm not telling you my name so as to help you to realize that." The renderings in various Bible versions indicate the elusiveness of the meaning:

"My name . . . is beyond understanding" (NIV), "too wonderful" (NRSV), "you wouldn't understand if I told you" (NLT), "it is too amazing for you to understand" (NCV) and so on (v. 18). Then Manoah and his wife offered a sacrifice to the Lord, who, though they did not yet know it, was in fact their visitor. In the Old Testament there appears from time to time this mysterious figure identified as the angel of the Lord, who is spoken of in a way that shows him to be God in some sense acting as his own messenger. Shortly we shall find Manoah himself saying, "We have seen God!" (v. 22). I think the theologians have been right to suppose that this angel (the term means "messenger" in both Hebrew and Greek) was a preincarnate appearance of the Son of God, the personal divine Word whom we know as Jesus Christ our Lord. Be that as it may, as the flame of the sacrifice went up, the visitor ascended (so it's put in v. 20), that is to say, he rose out of sight actually in the flame.

Now imagine yourself standing alongside Manoah and his wife and watching that happen. The visitor who a moment ago was beside them has suddenly, somehow, moved into the flame of the burnt offering, and he's literally going up in it. And now he's vanished. It was, I suppose, the experience of a fleeting moment, which left them wondering if they could believe their eyes at the same time as it dropped them facedown to the ground in instinctive awe. What's happened? They found it traumatic. So, I think, would you and I have done if we'd been there.

But this was God in action, and from the event we immediately learn that knowing God is not just a matter of doctrinally sound cognition regarding God, or of thorough-going commitment to God, or of personal, disciplined communion with God, or of peaceful contentment in God (although it includes all those things), nor is it just a matter of focusing on Christ as the way to

God and as your Savior, your Lord, your Friend, your Mediator, your Hope and your Joy—though it includes all of that too. With and beyond all that has been mentioned, knowing God is a matter of being ready for the surprises.

Manoah's Reaction

Manoah and his wife had a traumatic surprise. Let us focus on them and observe how each reacted to it—for their reactions were very different and very revealing. Look first at Manoah.

I know Manoah, and in fact I'm sure you do. He's a human type, as familiar today as ever. Correct behavior, as an ideal, is for him the essence of what life is about. He is religious, conscientiously so, but he views religion entirely as a matter of correctness in outward observances, and without quite recognizing what he is doing he treats these observances as a buffer between him and God, ensuring that God does not come too close. Deep down he is afraid of what the consequences for his life might be if his God, the God of Israel and of Christians, singled him out for attention. Meantime, however, he acts as the one who is and ought to be the man in charge and is reluctant ever to delegate, lest without him things would go wrong.

Is he ridiculous? Yes. Pompous? Yes. Fussy? Yes again. Distrustful of other people, his wife for instance? Oh yes, for sure. Just look how he behaves in this story. His wife comes to him (see Judg 13:6–7) and says, "This visitor, this man of God" (she thought she had met a prophet, you see) "came to me and what do you think he said? You know we've given up hope of having a family; well, he told me we're going to have a son." She then went through the specific instructions that she'd been given, namely, to prepare for the birth by avoiding alcohol and food that would defile her ceremonially, and never to cut her boy's hair once he was born, since he was to be a Nazirite—that is, a person specially dedicated to God for special services. (Details about the Nazirite commitment are in Num 6.) Then Manoah prayed, "O Lord, I beg you, let the man of God you sent to us come again to teach us how to bring up the boy who is to be born" (Judg 13:8). What that shows is that Manoah wouldn't trust his wife to get anything right. Manoah views himself as the man in charge, and he believes that God ought to speak directly to him, so he prays in terms that mean: "You know, Lord, I can't rely on the things she says, and this is important, so please let the man of God come to me and tell me what we're to do. Then I'll see to it that we obey instructions."

Do you get the picture? Manoah's attitude of I'm-the-only-one-who-can-do-things-right was a massive putdown of his wife. She had to endure being treated as incompetent, unreliable when she reported things and not fit to be trusted with any major decision or task. Was she happy in her marriage? I doubt it. Is this the biblical ideal of male leadership in marriage? I am sure it is not. But we cannot go into that here. Back to Judges 13.

Now God is very gracious, and when we pray, he meets us where we are, even if we're not in the place where we should be. So we read that God heard Manoah, and the angel of the Lord came again. He appeared once more to Mrs. Manoah. There's a gentle rebuke in that. Manoah had asked, "Let him come to me." But no, God comes again to the woman. So the woman, loyal spouse that she is, runs to her husband and says, "The man of God is back. Come and meet him." And Manoah goes and meets the visitor and says very gruffly, "Are you the person who talked to my wife?" Manoah, remember, is conscientious about what he sees as correct, and his words expressed a stuffy kind of protectiveness, as if to say, "You shouldn't talk to my wife. You should talk to me. It's not right for you to put her under strain by telling her things that she's then got to tell me." Do you get the nuance? He's babying the woman! That's the truth. But he's that sort of man. And Mrs. Manoah is locked into that sort of marriage.

"Are you the person who talked to my wife?" Manoah asks. "Yes, indeed I am," says the visitor. So Manoah asks his question in the most courteous Eastern way, "Yes, of course your words are going to be fulfilled. No question about that. But when they're fulfilled, what's to be the rule for the boy, for his life and work? Tell me." And the angel of the Lord says, "Well, it's exactly as I said to your wife. Your wife must do all that I told her." The gentle rebuke of Manoah's mistrust is still there, but the angel then details the instructions as Manoah had asked him to do. Then Manoah, who as we saw is a religious man and wants to do everything right, says, "Now, may we have a party in your honor since you've brought us this good news?" And the angel of the Lord replies, "No, I'll not stay to party, but it would be a good idea to offer a sacrifice to God." So Manoah does that; in celebration and thanksgiving he sets up a large sacrifice on a rock altar nearby and puts a match to it.

Manoah's Dread

And then came the traumatic sight that knocked Manoah completely off balance and showed that his religion was only a surface-level affair. Manoah did not know how to cope with the reality of the divine approach, and he panicked, as we can see from his words recorded in Judges 13:22. Manoah realized that his visitor was the angel of the Lord, and he cried out to his wife, "We are doomed to die! We have seen God!"

Now Manoah had hold of a half-truth at that point. He realized that neither he nor his wife was fit by nature to fellowship with God. What is reflected in Manoah's words was his sense that God is, in truth, *holy:* pure, just and strong, intolerably se-vere, terrifyingly hostile to evil and imperfection, and inexora-ble once he detects things that are wrong. There's a truth there—although it was a superstitious panic that Manoah was expressing, a fear that lost sight of the fact that God himself in-stituted the sacrificial system so that the destructive force of his holiness reacting to sin might not jeopardize his own peo-ple. But what Manoah said here shows that his religion was only skin-deep, a formality based on fear rather than a fellowship based on faith, and such religion is not good enough for anyone. To live on the surface, going through conventional routines of worship but without ever having thought in detail about what knowing God and living with God might involve you in or re-quire of you, is insufficient. That was all the religion that Manoah had and at a time when something had come out of the blue that he'd never dreamed of and that had given a profound shock to his spiritual system, this religion simply failed him. Hope fled. He thought they were both going to die—and said so, inviting his wife to agree with him.

The truth is that, both humanly and spiritually speaking, Manoah had lost his head. People constantly do when, under God's sovereignty, unnerving circumstances and traumatic trou-bles that they never expected come out of the blue. At such times Manoah-like thoughts form in the mind, and people jump to the conclusion that the fact of this happening to them shows that God has turned against them. "I thought he would protect me from all upheavals and give me a quiet, sheltered life, but I was wrong. He cannot love me after all. I'm doomed to die. The light is out. All my hope is gone." Logical thinking? No. Emotional thinking? Yes. Natural thinking? For many hangers-on in and around the churches, members of what we may call the Manoah club, yes again. A second-hand religion without first-hand knowledge of God will be valued mainly as a stabilizer, and so will be vulnerable to any kind of shock.

A Sensible Wife

That's Manoah. Please contrast him now with Mrs. Manoah. She also is a human type I know well. She is shy and quiet. She is self-effacing, ordinarily staying in the background. She lives with the constant putdowns that flow from Manoah's pomposity and passion for control and unwillingness to trust other people. She does not enjoy them but has learned to endure them. She is a faithful wife. When the angelic visitor appeared to her, she was scared, but she listened carefully to him and then went straight to tell her husband, to whom she reported the visitor's message with perfect accuracy. Manoah's assumption that he could not rely on her account of what was said was one more insult, but she bore it without complaint. Now when Manoah her husband, having taken over in his bossy way, has lost his head, she quietly chides him in a way that shows that, low-key, fearful and diffident though she is, she's a truly spiritual person with a heart firmly anchored in God himself and a depth that her husband lacks. She is indeed one of the great women of the Bible, as her words in Judges 13:23 show. I amplify them to bring out their force.

"Manoah," she says, "if the LORD had meant to kill us here and now, he would not have accepted a burnt offering or a grain offering from our hand, and he has in fact just accepted both. He would not in that case have shown us all these things that he has now shown us, nor told us that we're going to have a son. That certainly means that, far from killing us, he is instead going to keep us alive for nine months at least. He's perfectly consistent. He stands by his purposes; he fulfills his promises. I've had a shock to my system, Manoah, just as you've had a shock to yours. But our God is God the Faithful One, wise, rational, steady and safe for us to trust, and that's what we must hold on to as we seek to get our breath back after what we've seen."

These are the words of a person who truly knows God and has kept her head. In this she is a model for us. We too are likely to experience startling surprises as we seek to walk with God. Kipling's poem "If " begins with the words "If you can keep your head when all around you/Are losing theirs, and blaming it on you . . ." and goes on in that vein until each verse ends with the words, "You'll be a man, my son." That masculine pronoun, of course, is Kipling being Edwardian in the days when no one complained at the use of the generic "man" to include women, like Mrs. Manoah. What Kipling is talking about is maturity as such. And what we see here in the text is spiritual maturity, maturity in the knowledge of God. I'm urging that Mrs. Manoah showed spiritual maturity and depth in a way that enabled her to minister significantly to her husband, who ordinarily was unwilling to treat her as an equal or to take anything from her. Now I say to my fellow males, when we have the blessing of life partners, whatever we make of the creation pattern for husband and wife together, we must never be so proud that we won't let our wives minister to us when we need to be ministered to and they have the resources to do that. I am bold to affirm it part of God's order that wives should minister to their husbands just as their husbands should minister to them, and woe betide the husband who refuses to recognize that sometimes he needs that.

Coping with Surprise

Mrs. Manoah knew what her husband's problem was, and she

ministered to him accordingly. He needed to hear what she had to say to him, and it looks as if God used her thinking faith to restore his sinking heart. My guess is that the writer of Judges 13 smiled a bit, as we smile too, at some of the details of the story he had to tell. We are allowed to smile at some of the things in the Bible. Pomposity punctured always has a comic side.

But this is a narrative with some serious lessons for us. For we too, like Manoah, may think we are well on top of spiritual matters and then experience a traumatic shock that will show us up as spiritually shallow, because the first thoughts that surface after the shock will be neither scriptural nor faithful (faith-full, I mean), nor indeed rational. Instead, as we saw, we may find ourselves saying to ourselves and perhaps to others too, "God has turned against me; he has broken his word; he has let me down; he has forgotten me; there is no hope for me now." These devastating and despairing and self-pitying notions slander God as well as crush us, and when we find them going through our minds, we shall need someone with the spiritual depth and clear-headedness of Mrs. Manoah to put us straight.

For though our God remains a God of surprises, and though in the short-term some of his surprises hurt us and take our breath away, the final surprise to which all the rest are leading is the happy surprise of more good for ourselves and others, more joy, more wisdom, more contentment and more exultation in God, resulting from the times of trauma, than ever we thought possible: just as the end product of Manoah's encounter with God was the birth of Samson to a couple who had given up all hope of ever having a family. The principle that operates is well-focused in the familiar hymn "How Firm a Foundation":

> Fear not, I am with thee, O be not dismayed;
> For I am thy God, and will still give thee aid;

I'll strengthen thee, help thee, and cause thee to stand,
Upheld by my righteous, omnipotent hand.

When through the deep waters I call thee to go,
The rivers of grief shall not thee overflow;
For I will be with thee in trouble to bless,
And sanctify to thee thy deepest distress.

The full fruitage of coping through Christ with experiential earthquakes and thunderbolts will only be realized in the life to come, but already those with eyes to see begin to discern it both in themselves and in others. "God disciplines us for our good, that we may share in his holiness. No discipline seems pleasant at the time, but painful. Later on, however, it produces a harvest of righteousness and peace for those who have been trained by it" (Heb 12:10–11).

Manoah's experience of seeing God was meant to draw him closer to God in his own heart at a deeper level than he had known before. Emotional thinking, evidently the product of unreasoning fear that constantly pervaded his soul (for those whose passion, like his, is for correctness, regularly turn out to be running scared), nearly kept this from happening. But God evidently used Mrs. Manoah's word of wisdom to help him over the hump of panic and desperation, so that proper hope took up residence in his heart, and no doubt Manoah became a stronger saint for the experience.

One lesson we should learn then from watching what happened to Manoah is that central to the fulfilling of the biblical command to watch over our hearts (the heart being the inner core of our personhood, the source of all our attitudes and energies) is the discipline of watching over our heads. By this I mean that we must understand God's revealed ways with his children well enough not to be shattered by sudden, jolting surprises, and we must always

offer back to God the circumstances that baffle our brains so that
he may sanctify them, rather than let them become a reason for
giving up hope in God—as Manoah was in danger of doing.

A Memorable Woman

And what of Mrs. Manoah? The story suggests, as we saw, that it
was her husband's habit to treat her not as a fully rational, fully
trustworthy adult partner in their marriage, but rather as one
would treat a growing girl whose competence one doubted and
whom therefore one sought all the time to guide with one's own
fancied wisdom. If this was so, life for her was one prolonged putdown, and like Ibsen's Nora in *A Doll's House,* she must have felt
it, even though, unlike Nora, she could do nothing about it.
There is no reason to think that Manoah's recovery of faith
through her words changed the dynamics of their marriage. So
how should we assess this lady? Three things stand out.

First, she knew God. Trusting the goodness of the God of Israel
gave her a frame of understanding within which she could handle
the fear she felt when the visitor first confronted her (Judg 13:6)
and then not yield to the fear Manoah felt when it appeared that
the visitor was God in person. It enabled her to keep her head at
the moment of crisis and infer that since God willed, nine
months or more down the road, to give them a son who would
become Israel's savior from the Philistines, and since he had accepted the burnt offering, that is, the blood sacrifice that he had
told them to offer to God (remember, blood in the sacrificial system was always for the covering of sin; see Lev 17:11), he could
not be planning to strike them dead at that moment—as Manoah
felt he must be. She hoped in God because she was, in Old Testament terms, a believer. Faith shows itself in hope.

Second, she accepted her situation. She was loyal to her husband, Manoah, even when his attitude toward her left something to be desired. She ran to share with him what the visitor had said, since it concerned him as much as it concerned her, and she did not complain when, in his overbearing way, he assumed leadership and sidelined her, as he had so often done before. She must have offered the abrasiveness of this to God long since and asked for strength to sustain the marriage without bitterness or self-pity, and evidently she had been given what she sought. In her quiet way she was a holy woman and a good wife. Holiness shows itself in patient goodwill.

Third, she ministered to Manoah despite his habit of not taking her seriously as a partner. She spoke truth in love to him because that was what he needed. Guided in what she said and did by the needs of others, she was a ministering woman. The ministering mindset shows itself by constantly seeking to help.

A great woman! A woman honored, sustained and used by God! And one to imitate, as God the Holy Spirit enables, in her faith and hope, contentment and love, self-control and service.

Almighty Father, God whose name is wonderful, and secret and beyond our understanding—just because in your plans and purposes for us there is so much more than ever we guess at this moment, draw near to us now through the Holy Spirit, we pray. Write the word of your faithfulness in our hearts. Send our minds back to your gift to us of Jesus the Lord to be our Savior: the pledge of your love and the pledge of your faithfulness too. Convince us then, Holy Father, that we may trust you and hope in you, in all circumstances because you will stand to your purposes in consistency. And you will in due time fulfill all your promises to us even though there are moments when the roof falls in and everything seems to be going wrong. So, Holy Father, may we in the short-term learn our lessons from the shortcomings of

*Manoah and the faithful wisdom of his wife, and come to know
you in spiritual depth and true maturity to our blessing and to
your glory; for Jesus' sake. Amen.*

Study

1. What are some ways that you respond to unexpected events?

2. Read Judges 13:1–25. In what ways would this visit from "the angel
of God" change the lives of Manoah and his wife?

3. What reasons did they have to be frightened about this visit? To be
joyful?

4. Why do you think the angel of God came to the woman both times?

5. What does the conversation between the woman, the man and the
angel reveal about the relationship between Manoah and his wife?

6. What hints of yourself do you see in Manoah? In Mrs. Manoah?

7. Study verses 16–20. What can Manoah and his wife know about God
from this experience?

8. God is a surprising God. What do you not know about him?

9. Review the section of this chapter titled "Coping with Surprise" (pp.
67-70). How might the story of Manoah and his wife help you cope with
life's surprises?

10. God blessed Manoah with a sensible and spiritually discerning
wife. Who within your own circle of acquaintances possesses similar
characteristics? How can you respectfully draw on those strengths?

Pray

■ "Why do you ask my name?" said the angel of the Lord, "It is beyond
understanding." Pray, praising God for who he is—even for those aspects
that you cannot fully understand.

■ Prayerfully consider whether some of Manoah's flawed characteristics
are also a part of your own being, for example, an inordinate desire to
control, the tendency to "catastrophize," a way of speaking disrespect-
fully to someone in your family, a failure to trust in the goodness of God.
Confess to God any flaws or sins in these areas, ask his forgiveness, and
seek spiritual vigor from him to overcome these traits.

■ By comparing the information in Judges 13:1 with verses 24–25, we can see that God's design surrounding the events of this chapter was more complex and far-reaching than either Manoah or his wife could imagine. Pray, acknowledging the limitations of your own view as you encounter surprising episodes of your life. As much as you are able, express your trust in the Master Designer.

■ Read aloud to God the closing prayer of this chapter, making it personal by inserting the words *I* and *me* where appropriate.

Write

How has God surprised you? Probably you have not held a conversation with the "angel of the Lord," only to see him disappear upward in the flames of an offering. But God does surprise us with unexpected events in our lives—and with evidence of his presence during those events. Write about one of those surprise events. Then describe ways that God revealed himself during that time.

4

HOPE WHEN I AM ANGRY WITH PEOPLE AND WITH GOD

Jonah

SUPPOSE I ASKED, "WHAT IS THE BOOK OF JONAH ABOUT?" WHAT would you answer? A lot of people, I think, would say simply, "It's about a man who was swallowed by a whale." And that of course is true, assuming that the "great fish" in Jonah 1:17 was a whale (that can be doubted), but it isn't the whole of the story. Really the whale is not the major matter in the book of Jonah at all.

This book is about a man and his God, a merciless man and his merciful God. But even to say it that way is backwards. C. S. Lewis wrote a book in the Narnia series called *The Horse and His Boy*, which was the right order for that story. (If you've read the book, you know that the horse Bree is the hero.) Similarly, the right way round to state the theme of the book of Jonah is to say that it's a story of our merciful God and his merciless man. What we see in the book is God teaching Jonah, the merciless man, two lessons that he badly needed to learn. We may say at once that Jonah would have been lost spiritually if he hadn't learned them.

Two Lessons

The first lesson is one of obedience. In Jonah 1:1–3, we read:

> The word of the LORD came to Jonah son of Amittai, "Go to the great city of Nineveh and preach against it, because its wickedness has come up before me." But Jonah ran away from the LORD and headed for Tarshish. He went down to Joppa, where he found a ship bound for that port. After paying the fare, he went aboard and sailed for Tarshish to flee from the LORD.

God had called Jonah to be a prophet: a man charged to run God's errands and deliver God's messages. The story begins with Jonah refusing to do that, and he has to learn the lesson of obedience. God uses the great fish to teach him that lesson. That is what the first two chapters deal with.

But then there's a second lesson. Jonah is a hard man, stony-hearted and merciless—and he has to learn the lesson of compassion. We watch God teaching him that lesson and using, this time, not a great fish but a little worm in order to do it. That is what the last two chapters cover.

Imperfect Servants

This is a story for all of us. God doesn't always pick the nice men and the nice women. In fact, it's just the opposite. It is God's way to choose and to use flawed human material. God picks sinners; God saves sinners; God calls, equips and uses sinners—and Jonah was one such sinner.

The Bible gives us life stories of many persons whom God chose and called to his service. Again and again it takes time out to tell us of the weaknesses, moral lapses and spiritual failures in their lives. God's way with these folk is to change them as he uses them and to use them while he's remaking them. Again and again the story is of God receiving glory through the service that is rendered, while at the same time the man (or woman) rendering it is very imperfect as yet. But God teaches them lessons about right living as he continues to use them. Sanctification and service go together. Sanctification advances while service proceeds.

Vancouver's new airport is fully in service, though on-site construction has not ceased since it opened, and God's reconstruction of believers' characters is carried through in the context of their regular ministry to others. This is God's way.

We see sanctification and service linked in the story of Jonah. We must realize that God tells us this and other such stories for our encouragement. You know as well as I do the misery that comes to a believer, one who's truly committed to the Lord, when you say or do something unworthy, and it's too late to change what you've done or to pull back the words. Your heart says, "There you go again. That's your weakness coming out as it so often does. You are a poor specimen of a Christian. You are not fit to serve the Lord. You blow it over and over and over." The book of Jonah tells us that our God is a God who chooses people who blow it but that he forgives them for blowing it, and he works with them and on them to reduce their liability to lapse as they formerly did. And he uses them all the same. He gives us the privilege of serving him, despite all our deficiencies. Constantly he blesses things that we say and do—even though we blot our own copy book time after time. Our God is a gracious God, and this is just one expression of his goodness. That graciousness of God gives us the wavelength to tune into as we explore the book of Jonah.

Jonah's Motives

Look first at the merciless man, Jonah the uncaring prophet. He
was a Jew in the Northern Kingdom in the days of Jeroboam II,
whose military success in restoring Israel's former boundaries
Jonah had been privileged to predict (1 Kings 14:25). He clearly
was, to put it in positive terms, a patriot whose affection was
focused on his own people. To put it in negative terms, he was a
racist—he had a hostile attitude toward people of nationalities
other than his own, especially, as his story shows, the Assyrians.
An Ulster loyalist, with his hard-shell religio-political negativism
toward Roman Catholics, might be something of a modern parallel.

One of the interesting things in the book of Jonah is that nearly
every time God is spoken of, he is referred to by the covenant
name that he had given to the Jews, the name whereby they
were to invoke him, and in terms of which they were to know,
love and trust him. That name used to be rendered Jehovah;
scholars now pronounce it Yahweh. In our English translations
it's the LORD (in small caps). In this book of forty-eight verses the
name appears twenty-six times. The Jews thought of themselves
as the only people who knew their Maker as a God who loves and
saves and was in covenant with them, and the Old Testament
writers intend to bring this divine commitment to their readers'
minds every time they speak of God as "the LORD." To a crew of
polytheistic sailors of various nationalities, who between them
worshiped a wide range of gods, Jonah declared: "I am a Hebrew
and I worship the LORD, the God of heaven, who made the sea
and the land" (Jon 1:9). The strength and exclusiveness of this
Jewish identity is the starting point of the book's story.

What now of Nineveh? The capital of Assyria, Nineveh was a
large city, and Assyria was a great nation. Nineveh in Jonah's day,

which was the eighth century before Christ, was up and coming. Its size, influence and military might made it the leading imperial power of the day and a constant threat to the Jews in Israel.

If I may offer another modern parallel, mainland China gives Taiwan the feeling of being threatened by a very powerful neighbor, and that was how Israelites in Jonah's day felt about Nineveh.

When God says to Jonah, "Go to the great city of Nineveh and preach against it, because its wickedness has come up before me" (Jon 1:2), the prophet knows what that means. It's not God simply sending a message to Nineveh to the effect that it's all up with you. The first verse of chapter 4 says that Jonah was greatly displeased and became angry. You may wonder why. The answer is, because when he delivered God's message to Nineveh, Nineveh repented. We are told that when "God saw what they did, and how they turned from their evil ways, he had compassion and did not bring upon them the destruction he had threatened" (3:10). By verse 2 of chapter 4, Jonah is praying thus: "O LORD, is this not what I said when I was still at home? That is why I was so quick to flee to Tarshish. I knew that you are a gracious and compassionate God, slow to anger and abounding in love, a God who relents from sending calamity." "And that's what you've done here!" we can hear Jonah complain.

In other words, says Jonah, "I knew that if I went to Nineveh and delivered your message of judgment, you might use it as you've used messages and threats of judgment so often before. You use such preaching to bring people to repentance, you use it to bring them to their senses, you use it to make them humble themselves before you and change their ways—and then you forgive them. And I didn't want that to happen in Nineveh. That's why I didn't want to go to Nineveh and deliver your message."

God's grace to Nineveh seemed disgraceful to Jonah, a soft-hearted lapse from what God ought to have been doing, and Jonah's running away to Tarshish had really been the prophet's attempt to save God from himself.

The Jonah in Us

Jonah at least is an honest man, and here he is spelling out in his prayers exactly how he feels about the way God has acted. He hates to think of the use God has made of his own prophetic ministry, and in his disgust he tells God that in view of that he would rather be dead than alive. "Now, O LORD, take away my life, for it is better for me to die than to live" (Jon 4:3). As we can see, Jonah is a proud man and a bitter man, and at this moment he's an exceedingly angry man.

Let's pause now and think. I could be writing to a Jonah: someone who is proud, stiff, who doesn't bend, who throws his weight about, who is bitter at what he would describe as the tricks life has played on him. He is fiercely loyal to causes, some of them very good causes, but he's got no love in him for needy people. He's not merciful; he's hard, even fanatical. And so he's not a good man to appeal to when you're in trouble and in need because he never has anything for you. It is principles, rather than people, that stir him to action. He is passionate in his patriotism, or whatever form his idealism takes, but aloof and cold-hearted in personal relationships. Abstract goals get him excited; individuals in distress leave him unmoved.

Now he's angry. There are many people these days who carry a great tankful of anger around inside them. You never know when it's going to break out, when these people are going to lash out in fury. Often it is quite trivial things that stir up their anger. If you are the object of that anger, it may not have been anything to do with you—but you are there, and they feel mad and just have to let it boil over. And in their rage they say wild, irrational, irrelevant, insulting things constantly. Jonah is an angry man, angry with God, letting his anger overflow against God for what God has done. Do you recognize him? Have you met him? I think all of us are Jonah to some extent. Remember that as we look further at his story.

Going Away from God

Back now to the beginning. We know what Jonah did. God said, "Go to Nineveh," which was due east from Jerusalem. And Jonah in both senses of the phrase (geographical and evaluative) went west—for Tarshish is a port in Spain as far away from Nineveh as you could imagine. Thus Jonah gritted his teeth and said, "Nineveh? I'm not going to go." The NIV rendering is that he "ran away from the LORD" (Jon 1:3). The Hebrew says that he went out from God's *presence*, and that gives you a thought that you can't get from the NIV translation. The presence of the Lord is something very precious. It is not a geographical but a covenantal reality. It is, precisely, knowing that God is with you to bless you wherever you are. When Jonah ran away from the Lord in disobedience, Jonah, I think, knew that he was running away from the blessing of God. It was a sort of spiritual suicide. But I suppose he thought of it as a brave gesture. He didn't want any chance of Nineveh repenting; he wanted Nineveh to be judged. The happiest thing for Israel, he thought, would be to see Assyria go up in flames; so he defies God by refusing to preach there. He saw himself as a hero, sacrificing himself for his people's welfare. But it was idiocy, really. He was leaving the presence of the Lord. He was turning his back on God, and God on his throne in glory will not have his purposes thwarted by action like this. There is no future for anyone trying to be wiser than God, or to stop him from doing what he plans.

So Jonah went out, bought his ticket for the Tarshish boat and sailed for Tarshish to flee from the Lord. He went out, and by going out in this way he lost out most definitely. He lost out because, before the ship had gone very far, it was caught in a storm that, Scripture tells us, God himself raised. Verse 4 says, "The LORD sent a great wind on the sea, and such a violent storm arose that the ship threatened to break up."

God's Confrontation

Jonah is at this time (fairly soon after leaving port) slumbering between decks somewhere. I imagine that he lost a good deal of sleep in making his suicidal decision to disobey God. God in his kindness usually doesn't let us sleep well after we've made disastrous decisions like this. But Jonah is so tired that he is able to sleep and to go on sleeping despite the storm. He's on a pagan boat with an international crew, all the sailors are praying aloud, each one to his own god, and the captain goes down and finds Jonah asleep and says, "Get up and call on your god!" The captain assumes, as polytheists do, that the more gods that can be persuaded to involve themselves in a situation of need, the better it will be, since the amount of supernatural help will thereby be increased. Everybody therefore should call on the god whom he thinks he knows best. "We call on our gods," he says to Jonah, "you call on your god. Let's see if somehow we can get the help we need from somewhere by calling on all the deities there are."

Jonah, in fact, undoubtedly can't pray because of his refusal to obey God, and he explains this to the captain and the sailors. That is clear from the last sentence in 1:10: "They knew he was running away from the LORD, because he had already told them so." And I imagine that was what he told the captain: "I can't pray because I've turned my back on my God." To know and feel that you cannot persuade God to listen to you about anything because you have chosen to quarrel with him about something is an awful position for anyone to be in. But at least Jonah is honest in his spiritual madness, and he tells it like it is.

So now they cast lots, asking all the gods they know to show them who is responsible for their trouble. The lot falls on Jonah. They assume, rightly as it turns out, that the storm is a sign of divine displeasure at someone on the ship itself. The whole crew is down there, I suppose, below deck, hanging on to things as the ship rolls; they are scared and angry. They say to Jonah, "It has to be you. What have you done to bring this storm on us?"

Jonah tells them, "It's because I've turned my back on my God. I'm a Hebrew. I worship the LORD, the God of heaven—only I don't at the moment. I've run away from him. He gave me a commission that I wasn't prepared to fulfill." The sea is getting rougher so they say, "What should we do to you to make the sea calm down for us?" Jonah is brave in his spiritual ruin. He says, "You'd better throw me overboard." He's been found out, and now he's going to be thrown out—in the most literal sense. And they do it. Jonah flies through the air into the heaving sea, expecting to drown.

Let us learn from this how ruinous a thing it is to defy God and imagine that we can get away with refusing to do his will. God is in his heaven; God is on the throne; God is fully in charge of his world. No one can get away with defying God, and Jonah didn't get away with it.

God's Mercy
Being thrown overboard would have been the end of Jonah but

for the mercy of God. So let us shift the focus now from the merciless man whose path downhill we've followed to think about the merciful God whom Jonah served and whose mercy as a caring Creator is shown over and over in this book. We begin to see this in Jonah 1:15: "They took Jonah and threw him overboard, and the raging sea grew calm." The storm died down at once. The crew had not wanted to do what they did and had prayed to Jonah's God (of whose reality, it seems, Jonah's sad story had convinced them) asking that the action to which Jonah directed them would not be held against them. Now the effect of the stilling of the storm was that the crew "greatly feared the LORD, and they offered a sacrifice to the LORD, and made vows to him" (v. 16). This is an Old Testament way of saying they were converted through the work of the Holy Spirit in their hearts. They had really come to know and serve the real God. That was mercy from God to this pagan crew.

Now let's look at Nineveh, where God showed mercy again. In chapter 3 we see how the story went. Jonah proclaimed, "Forty more days and Nineveh will be overthrown" (Jon 3:4). He didn't say anything to them about the possibility of mercy, but God moved in their hearts just as he had moved in the hearts of the pagan crew and so we read in verse 5, "The Ninevites believed God. They declared a fast, and all of them, from the greatest to the least, put on sackcloth." The king of Nineveh led them, issuing a proclamation (see vv. 7–9) saying that everybody must share in the fast. Man and beast must be covered with sackcloth. The royal decree said, "Let everyone call urgently on God. Let them give up their evil ways and their violence." This was the king of Nineveh himself calling the Assyrians to repentance. "Who knows," his proclamation continues, "God may yet relent and with compassion turn from his fierce anger so that we will not perish." And God did. There was a grand-scale revival, as we might call it, and Nineveh survived.

So here again is God being merciful. Jonah, wanting Assyria destroyed, was disgusted, but he should not have been, nor should we ever allow ourselves to wish destruction on others and long to see it, as he did. Whenever you feel hostile to anybody or any group of people, however badly they may have behaved toward you, stop and remember, and say to yourself: God made them, as God made me. God loves them, as God loves me. If they turn to Christ, they'll be forgiven, as I am forgiven. It's not my part to cherish hostility toward them because of what I see as their sins when my Savior-God has shown such wonderful redemptive love toward sinful me. This is an element in the Christian mindset that you learn in experience, by making yourself think along these lines, namely, to love your enemies as well as your friends and to desire God's best for the one category as well as the other. Loving your neighbor includes enemies as well as friends. It's a tremendous lesson, and it takes all of life for some of us to learn it. Some perhaps never learn it. Some perhaps are very slow to realize that they need to learn it. But we all must learn it. The story of revival in Nineveh rubs our noses in the fact that God is supremely glorified when he shows himself merciful—even to those who up to this point have acted as his enemies. The Lord Jesus on his cross was praying, "Father, forgive them, for they do not know what they are doing." He was praying for the soldiers who at that time were nailing him to the cross (Lk 23:34). To be merciful to enemies and wrongdoers, and to desire and seek their welfare is, in truth, central to the real Christian life.

Jonah and God's Mercy

Now look at Jonah again and see how God was merciful to him.

The Lord prepared the great fish to swallow Jonah up, but he didn't lose consciousness straightaway. When he found himself inside the fish, spiritually he came to his senses. Thoughts went through his mind, and humble, hopeful, thankful, trustful prayer came out of his heart—which (later, one supposes) he turned into the psalm in Jonah 2:1–9. Soon we read, "The LORD commanded the fish, and it vomited Jonah onto dry land." You can imagine him staggering to his feet in the shallows and stumbling out of the water and then sitting down gasping and panting and realizing what had happened. It was not just that God had saved Jonah's life; God had shown his hand; God had taught his prophet a lesson; God had opened his heart; God had forgiven him for a ruinous bit of disobedience; God had restored him to godliness and now wished to restore him to his prophetic ministry. Awed at that moment by the marvel of God's majestic mercy, Jonah must surely have resolved never to say no to God again.

So when "the word of the LORD came to Jonah a second time: 'Go to the great city of Nineveh and proclaim to it the message I give you,'" Jonah obeyed (Jon 3:1–3). Now there's mercy! The prophet is back in business once more. God restores Jonah to ministry, and he blesses others through his ministry. Jonah, as we have seen, is very angry at this because he wanted to see Nineveh perish. But he should have been rejoicing! It isn't every preacher whose ministry brings revival blessing and who sees great numbers of folk turning to God as a result of the things he has proclaimed. That's what Jonah saw. And I say it was mercy, to the preacher as well as to the people.

Jonah's Anger

In chapter 4 we read how Jonah communed with God in great anger because God is, as he knows, "slow to anger and abounding

in love, a God who relents from sending calamity." God has acted
in character in dealing with the Ninevites. The irony and the
enormity of Jonah fisting up in anger with God because God has
not expressed anger with the objects of Jonah's anger needs no
underlining. We shall now watch as God interrogates Jonah, dip-
ping into both his head and his heart.

Jonah 4:4 tells us that God replied to Jonah, "Have you any
right to be angry?"—angry the way you are? Jonah in his own
conscience knows, or half-knows, that by this question God is rebuking him, but he won't yet accept it. This again is something
that all too often happens in our lives. We half-know that God is
prodding our conscience about something. But at first we aren't
willing to face it, and so we deliberately don't think about it. We
think about something else, or we go off and do something else.
Maybe for quite some time we will keep up our daily praying and
reading of God's Word, but we won't say anything to him about
this matter over which he's making us feel uneasy. But God, the
"hound of heaven" as with Francis Thompson we may call him,
gets us in the end. Sooner or later we have to face the issue that
he's pressing on us. It's mercy that God doesn't let us finally ignore that prodding of our conscience. Here for the moment,
however, Jonah is trying to ignore it—and God bides his time.

What does Jonah do? He goes outside the city and makes himself a shelter, a sort of lean-to shack. He sits in the shade and
waits and watches and hopes all the time that, despite the revival,
despite the repentance, despite his fears that God is resolved to
act in mercy, God will nonetheless destroy Nineveh. So he sits
there and gazes toward Nineveh hour after hour, hoping to see it
go up in flames. Remember, he's a patriot; he's a racist; he's a
proud and bitter man. Yes, he has a real faith, matured by his experience with the boat and the fish, but his character is sadly

wrong, and it hasn't changed yet. He's learned his lesson in obedience, but he hasn't yet learned his lesson of compassion.

God's Persistence

Now God moves in to teach him lesson number two. Jonah 4:6 says, "The LORD God provided a vine." Nobody quite knows what that "vine" was. Some translations say gourd, and some commentators describe it as a plant like a huge sunflower with big leaves and shade. The gourd—or vine or whatever it was—grew up quickly beside Jonah's lean-to. It gave Jonah "shade for his head to ease his discomfort, and Jonah was very happy about the vine. But then at dawn the next day God produced a worm, which chewed the vine" down at its roots so that the whole thing withered. "When the sun rose, God provided a scorching east wind, and the sun blazed on Jonah's head so that he grew faint. He wanted to die, and said, 'It would be better for me to die than to live'" (vv. 6–8).

Then God's word came to him in a way that couldn't be denied. "God said to Jonah, 'Do you have a right to be angry about the vine?'" (Jon 4:9).

"Yes, I do," says Jonah. "I'm so angry I could die. I needed that vine, and now you've taken it away."

Then God said (I expand the text of vv. 10–11), "You have been concerned about this vine although you didn't tend it or make it grow. It sprang up overnight and died overnight. But now think of Nineveh. Nineveh, in addition to its half-million and more adult inhabitants, has more than 120,000 young children and any number of cattle, and they're all mine. And if I am concerned, as I am, about the young children and the cattle, should it surprise you or offend you that I am also concerned about Nineveh's adult inhabitants? Don't you expect me to be concerned about what's mine? The vine was not really yours, but you were very concerned about it. It was more my vine, Jonah, than your vine, and yet you were angry enough when you lost it. Come now, don't you think that I'm right to show mercy to the penitent people of Nineveh? Do you imagine that I can sympathize with your anger at my mercy, Jonah? I certainly am angry with sinners and their sins, and there's wrath waiting for them if they don't leave their wrongdoings. But Nineveh has left its sins. Shouldn't I be glad of Nineveh's repentance and happy to acknowledge it by my gift of forgiveness?"

God's Lessons for Us

Thus God taught Jonah two key lessons: the lesson of obedience and the lesson of compassion. These are lessons our Lord wants us to learn and which everyone who serves the Lord must learn. As you and I live by being forgiven, as the Ninevites lived by being forgiven, and as Jonah himself lived by being forgiven, so let us appreciate God's saving mercy, which both lessons presuppose. As God taught Jonah the necessity of obedience in his service, so let us allow him to sensitize our consciences to the importance of always doing what he commands. As God set himself to change Jonah into a man of compassion, so let us allow him to teach us to be men and women of compassion, neighbor lovers in the fullest sense. Thus we shall truly become people who please him by consistently obeying his word, not stopping our ears to any assignment that we don't like. Let's learn to please God by trusting his wisdom as he puts us through corrective discipline to teach us these lessons. It was discipline for Jonah to be swallowed by the fish; it was discipline for Jonah to have his precious vine wither and fall at his feet. Through these experiences God was teaching Jonah. You and I must be willing to be taught also and to trust

God's wisdom as he deals with us, sometimes in a chastening way, to help us learn what he wants us to know.

Finally, all this must be set and seen in a Christ-centered, Spirit-oriented trinitarian frame. Let us learn then to love our neighbor, including our hostile and oppressive neighbors, by brooding on the way God in his love for us has acted for our salvation—yours and mine. "God so loved the world that he gave his one and only Son" (Jn 3:16). Jesus, you remember, spoke of the sign of Jonah, as he looked forward to his own death for our sins and his rising again to become the Savior who bestows new life. Jonah came back to life, as it were, from being inside the fish, and ministered to the Ninevites as living proof of God's determination to bring the word of judgment and mercy to them. So too the Son of Man came back to life in the power of his atonement to "preach peace" through the words of his servants to the world (Eph 2:17) and to become the living Mediator and Master of all who trust him. Let the impact of God, displayed in the ministry of Jesus, the one who was greater than Jonah, reshape us as the merciful, loving, outreaching people that all Christians are called to be.

Let us learn to be glad that our God, Jonah's God, is "a gracious and compassionate God, slow to anger and abounding in love, a God who relents from sending calamity" (Jon 4:2). Not only is he a mighty God, master of the wind and waves and giant fish, as well as of plants and little worms, but he is also a merciful God, calm and restrained in teaching truth and wisdom and goodwill to fanatical, merciless oddballs like Jonah in order to get them beyond their anger with him and their hard-heartedness with everyone else. Arrogance, anger and hopelessness go together: arrogance says to God, "my will be done"; anger says, "it is outrageous that you are not doing it, but doing the opposite"; the conclusion then drawn is "now everything will go wrong"—which is pure hopelessness, in spades, and the deepest motivation of Jonah's twice-repeated death wish (vv. 3, 8). Arrogance and anger must somehow be squeezed out of us before we can truly hope in God, practicing obedience as the good way for us and leaving global politics and history in his wise, generous and merciful hands—and this God does. In the book of Jonah we see him doing it for Jonah, and in that narrative lies the assurance that he will do it for us too. So let us Jonahs praise him and put ourselves in his hands for our remedial treatment.

O God, our heavenly Father, we are awed at the spectacle of your wisdom and patience with a difficult man that we find presented to us in the book of Jonah. We know that like him we too are called to become messengers of your mercy to lost souls, and like him, we erect barriers in our own hearts to the fulfilling of our mission. We know that we have in the past spoiled our service to you by our negativism on some things and our rigidity and pig-headedness on others, and we have closed our eyes and ears to the real needs of real people whom you have prompted us to go and seek to help. For the sake of Jesus, your Son, our Savior and example, forgive us Jonahs these ugly failings, and teach us to love the lost as you yourself do, so that the light and love of Christ may shine out in us as we go about your business. Melt us, mold us, break us, change us, use us, and yours shall be all the glory. Amen.

Study

1. Read the biblical book of Jonah.

2. What actions help reveal Jonah's character? What do you see of yourself in Jonah?

3. What examples do you see of the grace of God in Jonah's story?

4. Study Jonah's two descriptions of God in 1:9 and 4:2. In what ways did Jonah act on these stated beliefs? In what ways did his actions fail to live up to his beliefs?

5. Reread each of these descriptions of God with your own current circumstances in mind. What actions can you take that would live out this belief?

6. Of what value was the fish to Jonah?

7. When has a break in your own routine given you valuable insights from God?

8. In spite of Jonah's flaws, what good did God accomplish through him?

9. Jonah needed to learn two lessons: the lesson of obedience and the lesson of compassion. What measures did God use to teach those lessons?

10. How might you put one of Jonah's lessons to work in your own setting?

Pray

■ Spend a few moments in silence, reflecting on the life of Jonah. Ask God to reveal to you what he would like you to glean from Jonah's experience.

■ Reread the section titled "God's Mercy" (pp. 83-85). Worship God, praising him for his mercy. Then bring to mind God's specific acts of mercy in your own life and thank him for these.

■ Jonah complained in 4:2, "I knew that you are a gracious and compassionate God, slow to anger and abounding in love, a God who relents from sending calamity." Talk to God about your own response to these aspects of his character.

■ Reread the final paragraph of this chapter on pages 90-91. Use it as a basis for your own praying.

Write

Jonah's time inside a fish gave him opportunity to block out all distractions and get honest with God. (Most of us don't need a near drowning to experience this.) Create your own "fish" by purposely finding a time and place to communicate privately with God. Ask him to search your heart about the current direction of your life. (Are you appropriately obedient to God? Compassionate to others—even those you don't like?) Write out your prayer and meditation.

5

HOPE WHEN FALSE PRIORITIES HAVE BETRAYED ME

Martha

LUKE 10:38–42;
JOHN 11:1–44; 12:1–8

MARTHA THE SISTER OF MARY WAS A NATURAL-BORN TAKE-charge person, a manager by instinct. There is nothing wrong with that. We need such people, and life is not likely to go on well without them. They are often exuberant extroverts who take great pleasure in running things. The danger is that their managing may become manipulation, turning their service of others into self-service of a tyrannical type. Martha was not immune to that danger, as we shall shortly see.

We meet Martha first as a hostess. Jesus, we are told, came to a village where a woman named Martha opened her home to him (Lk 10:38). You know the state of mind in which you receive visitors into your home. What your heart says is, *This is my home. Welcome. I'm glad to see you here—but remember, I'm in charge.*

To be a host or hostess is to be in a managing role, and we see this clearly in Martha. Managing, as we said a moment ago, can be a problem, a stumbling block even, in the spiritual life. What we, like Martha, have to learn is that when we are sharing our life with our Lord Jesus Christ, we are not in charge. He's in charge. As we follow Martha through the three scenes where the Gospels show her in action, we shall see her learning this lesson. Many today seem to be saying to the Lord Jesus, "I'm glad you are in my life—but remember, I'm in charge." We forfeit much blessing and rob God of much glory if we take that line. Martha's story should point us in a different direction.

Martha Manipulating Jesus

Manipulation confronts us in this passage at the end of Luke 10. Here's what it says:

> As Jesus and his disciples were on their way, he came to a village where a woman named Martha opened her home to him. She had a sister called Mary, who sat at the Lord's feet listening to what he said. But Martha was distracted by all the preparations that had to be made. She came to Jesus and asked, "Lord, don't you care that my sister has left me to do the work by myself? Tell her to help me!"
>
> "Martha, Martha," the Lord answered, "you are worried and upset about many things, but only one thing is needed. Mary has chosen what is better." (I think the NIV makes a minor mistranslation here. The Greek says, "Mary has chosen what's necessary, what is good." Jesus is not making comparisons; his point is simply that there is supreme value in what Mary has chosen to do.) And Jesus continues, "It will not be taken away from her." (Lk 10:38–42)

What's going on here? Why is Jesus rebuking his hostess? Lest we misunderstand what we read, we should note right at the outset that it was not because Jesus had any kind of negative attitude toward women, as if he saw it as a male prerogative to use every opportunity to tell a woman she is in the wrong. Sometimes Christians are accused of viewing women as inferior to men, and it's alleged that the apostle Paul and the Lord Jesus are directly responsible for this. That's slander. It's totally false. The truth is the exact opposite. Jesus came into a world where pagan culture took for granted that women were inferior to men. Even in Jewish culture women were regarded as not on the same footing as men—although the Jewish mother was respected for her motherhood, and she was in charge in the home. But there was a prayer that young Jewish males were taught to pray, in which they thanked God that they had not been born a pagan or a slave or a woman. That says something! Yet Jesus welcomed women as disciples on exactly the same footing as he welcomed men. He had female friends, as he had male friends. He made no difference between them, and by this attitude he opened a new era for women in world history. He, and Paul after him, applying this attitude, did more to project women's worth and raise their status in community thought than any other two persons have ever done. We must not imagine that when Jesus rebukes Martha it's because he has an interest in putting a woman down. It's not that at all. He rebukes Martha because Martha actually has let herself down, and Jesus wants to make her into a better disciple than she was at that moment.

A little imagination will show us what is happening. It's Martha's home. That probably means that Martha is a widow, because under ordinary circumstances in ancient Palestine a woman wouldn't own property—but the widow regularly did. Martha has a sister named Mary who lives with her, and she has a brother named Lazarus, who also seems to live in the same home. On this day Martha has heard a knock at the door, gone to see who it was and found waiting there thirteen unexpected guests: Jesus and his twelve disciples. What does a good hostess do when she finds thirteen unexpected guests on the doorstep? Quietly and without making it obvious that this is a bit of a shock, she takes a deep breath and then says, "Why, how nice to see you all. Come in."

It's clear from the way Luke tells the story that Martha and Mary already knew Jesus. Hospitality, ordinarily overnight, often longer, was a standard and expected virtue in the ancient world. In the village of Bethany Jesus and his disciples knew that they could count on a welcome at Martha's home. Nowadays, when communications are so good, it would be bad manners for thirteen people to come to somebody's door without having at least made a phone call to alert the hostess to the fact that they're on their way. But there were no telephones in those days—no means of announcing their arrival in advance. So those who had homes had to be ready to welcome unexpected guests. Even so, thirteen must have seemed rather a large number.

But Martha is equal to it. She invites Jesus and his disciples in. They've been walking; they're tired; they sit down. And Jesus turns their rest hour into a teaching session. I suppose he sits rabbi-like, on a chair in the center of a semi-circle of his disciples—or maybe they're all sitting on the floor. Mary tiptoes in and sits down at one end of the semicircle. She wants to listen and to learn as well. So the teaching session goes on until suddenly there's an interruption. There behind the semicircle, glaring over the disciples' heads, is Martha with her hands on her hips. She's got a red face. She breaks into the conversation and says in a loud, strident, edgy voice, "Lord, don't you care that my sister has left me to do the work by myself? Tell her to help me."

She's blowing her top. She's making a scene. She's lost control. This is not good behavior by the hostess. She's letting herself down. Jesus is sharp with her, but as you will agree, I think, she needs his sharpness at this point.

If you look at Martha's words, she's really saying three things. One is that she wants to be noticed: *"Lord, don't you care that my sister has left me to do all the work by myself?* I am doing a lot of work. I'm preparing a meal for my thirteen uninvited guests. Do you realize that? Have you noticed?" There's a certain amount of both pride and self-pity in this. Martha wants Jesus' admiration and sympathy, and at that moment is not prepared to go on without it.

And there's more. *"Tell her to help me,"* says Martha. In these words there is a second thing. She wants to domineer her sibling, or putting it another way, she wants to run Mary's life for her. Mary lives in Martha's home, and Martha wants to be able to call the shots as to when Mary will come and help in the kitchen. You sometimes find this in families today. The elder brother or sister will try to set the agenda for the younger siblings and push them around and control their lives. For the younger siblings it can be a rough experience. In this instance I am sure that it was a rough moment for Mary. Can you imagine her looking at the floor and going very red in the face as she hears Martha say these things? I can.

Then there's a third thing—worst of all. Martha is actually trying to manipulate Jesus, to use Jesus as her heavy hammer for hitting sister Mary over the head. "Tell her to help me," she says. It's as if Martha is saying, "This sister of mine is such a rotten specimen that she wouldn't come if I simply sneaked up and tapped her on the shoulder and whispered 'I'm being run ragged in the kitchen—would you come and give me a hand?' No! You'll

have to tell her, Jesus." Martha is really blaming Jesus for the situation and trying to give him a sense of guilt about Mary's presence with the disciples so that he will jump to and order Mary
into the kitchen. Bad behavior? Well, yes. But Martha has lost
her temper. When we see red and blow our tops, we're on an ego
trip, we've lost control, and we say all sorts of wild things. That's
what's happening here, so you can't wonder that Jesus is rather
sharp with Martha. He has to calm her down, restore her balance
and refocus her sense of priorities. Watch how he does it.

Jesus Responds

The first thing communicated by Martha's words was that she
wanted to be noticed. Jesus' reply to her begins, "Martha, Martha, you are worried and upset about many things." In other
words: "Martha, you are noticed. I know what you're doing, and
I'm grateful. Don't be in any doubt about that." You and I should
bear in mind that our Lord Jesus always knows. He never forgets
those who are his. Though we may ourselves forget him, he
never in fact forgets us. He is wonderful that way. Martha's "don't
you care?" reminds us of when Jesus was asleep in the storm,
and the disciples woke him up with the same words (Mk 4:38);
on both occasions "yes, I care" was the answer implied by his
response. Out there in the kitchen preparing the meal, or perhaps making up thirteen extra beds somewhere in the building,
Martha ought to have been very sure that the Lord Jesus knew of
her efforts. But her self-pity has put that certainty out of her
mind. The Lord has to remind her that he knows, and he cares.

The second thing Martha had expressed was that she wanted
to control Mary's life by hauling her out into the kitchen. To that,
Jesus' response is, *"Mary has chosen what is good, and it will
not be taken away from her.* This is to say, Martha, that resent-

ing her absence from the kitchen is an attitude you shouldn't have; hauling her there is something you shouldn't be trying to do. You ought to be glad that Mary has the opportunity to sit here and listen to me and learn from me. You should think of it as your gift to her." In the same way you and I ought to be glad to give someone else the opportunity to learn the things of God from the Scriptures (which is how Jesus teaches his people nowadays). It's worth a little extra work on our part to give people that opportunity. This is clearly Jesus' thought as he reminds Martha that Mary is observing life's first priority.

The third thing that Martha had expressed in her words, as was said above, was a desire to manipulate and use Jesus as her tool against her sibling—in other words, her hammer for hitting Mary over the head. On that, Jesus is being quite firm with Martha. "Martha, you must not try to do that." This is what he implies when he says, "Only one thing is needed. Mary has chosen that good thing, and it will not be taken away from her. *I am not going to order her into the kitchen.*"

Mary and Martha by Turn

We must understand though that Jesus is not rebuking Martha for not being in the learning group, sitting beside Mary and letting him teach her the way that Mary is being taught. Had hostess Martha behaved that way, there never would have been any food on the table for any of them. Jesus approves of the fact that Martha is out in the kitchen making them a meal, just as he approves of the fact that Mary is there sitting at his feet and learning from him. Situational responsibilities are not to be ignored for the sake of devotional exercises, any more than vice versa. Martha has been doing the right thing for her in that situation, as has Mary, though they have been doing different things. The lesson that we all have to learn is to be Martha and Mary by turn. When the meal was made, it would be right for Martha to come in and join the party and learn from Jesus and deepen her relationship with him—just as Mary was doing. But until the requirements of hospitality were covered, Martha's place was backstage, doing what she had to do as Jesus' hostess.

Some have read Jesus' words as if Mary is being justified for not helping in the kitchen and Martha is being condemned for making the meal. I don't believe that either of those implications is right. Mary was called as part of God's will and of Christ's wish for her as his disciple, from time to time, to give Martha proper help in the house—but not at this particular moment. And Martha was called, once her hostess responsibilities were finished, to join Mary as Jesus' pupil, listening to his word and benefiting thereby. But Jesus was obliged to rebuke Martha because by her attitude both to Mary and to him, Martha had let herself down.

Let's learn then that we ought to have space in our lives for doing what Mary did: spending time with the Word of God, learning from Jesus by listening to him in worship and adoration—which is the most important activity of our life. But let us also learn that from time to time we are to be doing the practical helpful things that are needed around the house and for that matter around the church. Let us not suppose that intensity of devotion excuses us from this. Some of us skimp the Martha side of our discipleship, just as some of us skimp our times of Bible-reading and prayer—the Mary side of our discipleship. And skimping both ways is wrong. Our Lord Jesus looks for better than that from all of us.

The Death of Lazarus

Now let us look at another story about Martha. In John 11 we meet Martha and Mary again. Martha appears in this story in a much better light than in the story we just looked at, and we shall hear a wonderful confession of faith from her. Nonetheless, we shall find managerial Martha once more attempting to dictate the Savior's action and so in reality to obstruct Jesus in what he has come to do. It's a wonderful story, marvelously told, and I urge you to read it and reread it.

It is the story of the raising of dead Lazarus—one of the most amazing miracles that Jesus ever performed. It begins by telling us that Lazarus was desperately ill. Lazarus was the brother of Mary and Martha, and the sisters sent word to Jesus saying, "Lord, the one you love is sick" (Jn 11:3). That's a striking phrase: "the one you love." Clearly a close relationship has built up between Jesus and these three siblings: Lazarus and Martha and Mary. The event of John 11 took place probably two years later than that recorded in Luke 10. Jesus has no doubt been in Bethany from time to time since then, so his friendship with the trio has grown. In this context Jesus now learns that one of whom he has grown very fond is sick and dying.

Jesus, to the surprise of his disciples, who expected him immediately to go to Bethany and heal Lazarus, does not move for some days, not until in fact he knows, with his divine power of knowing at a distance, that his sick friend has died. Then at last they all go off to Bethany. The disciples have no idea what Jesus is going to do when he gets there. They're not expecting anything special. They can't understand why he's delayed. And Thomas, who was a bit of a pessimist I think from the things we're told about him, always looking on the gloomy side, said to the rest of the disciples (Jn 11:16), "Let us also go that we may die with him." *Him* may be Jesus, whose life was at risk in and near Jerusalem (see 10:31-39; 11:8), but I think *him* is Lazarus, and what

Thomas means is, "Well, he's dead. Let's go and at least share in the mourning, though we shall feel like death ourselves when we do." So the disciples were far from expecting a miracle now—but Jesus knew what he was going to do.

The Scene at Bethany

Jesus gets near Bethany, which is less than two miles from Jerusalem, and he is not far from the home where the two sisters and their brother lived. We read in John 11:20, "When Martha heard that Jesus was coming [I suppose someone ran ahead to the house and told her that he was on his way], she went out to meet him." When she met him, she said to him, "Lord, if you had been here, my brother would not have died." Martha is confident that in that case she would have seen one of Jesus' healing miracles. The next thing she said was, "But I know that even now God will give you whatever you ask." That was a roundabout, indirect and tentative way of saying, "Even now surely there's something you can do. Can you ask your Father to enable you to raise the dead? Surely you can, can't you?" She's not certain. She says, "I know," but more as a gesture of respect than as a confession of faith. Really she doesn't know. And she doesn't take seriously her own fantasy (at present it's no more than a fantasy) that Jesus might call Lazarus back from the dead. She doesn't pursue the thought when Jesus speaks to her of something else.

Martha's Confession

What Jesus does in response to Martha's poignant words of welcome, affirmation and wishful dreaming is probe to see what's in her heart. So he says, "Your brother will rise again. Do you know that?" Martha answers (and this is real strong faith and something very much to applaud), "I know he will rise again in the resurrection at the last day" (Jn 11:24). Martha was one of the godly Israelites who were sure of bodily resurrection to come. The Hebrews were divided on the subject of future resurrection: the Pharisees affirmed it; the Sadducees didn't. Jesus of course had taught from time to time about the coming resurrection, and Martha, Mary and Lazarus would no doubt have picked up that teaching from his own lips. Here then is Martha declaring with confidence what she has already learned from her Lord.

Then Jesus says to her something that she's not heard him say before, which she, like the rest of us, very much needs to learn, and which it seems she does learn as she hears him say it. Jesus tells her, "I am the resurrection and the life. He who believes in me will live, even though he dies [as Lazarus has died]; and whoever lives and believes in me will never die. Do you believe this?" (Jn 11:25–26).

That's what Jesus asks Martha. And she says in reply, "Yes, Lord, I believe." Now comes this magnificent confession, right, true and a model for us: "I believe that you are the Christ, the Son of God, who was to come into the world." As if to say, "You are God's Savior. You are our King. You are our hope. You have been sent by God to bring us life, and you yourself are more than human: in some way I feel and know you are divine." That's real faith in Martha's heart—just as it is real faith in us, if we are able to echo those words and have learned, like Martha, to seek Jesus' company. She has now learned to learn from him. We could almost say that she's being Mary. Martha is fulfilling that element of devoted discipleship to which she and Mary, like the rest of us, were called. She hears Jesus; she believes Jesus. "I am the resurrection and the life," Jesus says. "Yes, Lord," says Martha. "I believe that. You are God's Savior, and I believe that the one who trusts you in this life will always enjoy fellowship with you both here and hereafter. Such a person, I know, will have entered into eternal life—a life of fulfillment that knows no end." It's a great confession on Martha's part. Let us learn to trust Jesus in the way that she was trusting Jesus.

Martha's faith was the fruit of Jesus' probing and teaching. The confession he has drawn out of her reveals her as a magnificent believer. Now she goes back to the home and tells Mary that Jesus would like to see her. Mary comes up, and they all go to the tomb. Mary, who is in tears, says to Jesus just what Martha has said to Jesus: "Lord, if you had been here my brother would not have died" (Jn 11:32). But Mary isn't able to say anything more. She doesn't yet know, even as Martha really doesn't yet know, that Jesus can raise the dead. Mary's tears draw from Jesus a snort, or grunted exclamation, of outrage at the way death blights the goodness of God's world, and he asks to be taken to the tomb (vv. 33–34). So they go to the tomb, and some of the mourners who were with the two women in the house come to the tomb too. They are all weeping, and Jesus in compassion weeps with them (v. 35). And some of these friends say (v. 37), "Could not he who opened the eyes of the blind man have kept this man from dying?" They all know, more or less clearly, that Jesus can miraculously heal the sick. None of them as yet know with equal certainty that he can raise the dead, though they all privately wish he could. But revelation of that fact is on its way.

Obstruction Again

When they get to the rock tomb, Jesus says, "Take away the stone"—the massive boulder, that is, that's blocking the entrance. Martha doesn't understand why Jesus should say this. She supposes that he wants to view the body. We can understand her thinking that Jesus might want to take a last look at his friend who is now gone. But Martha, with her hostess mentality reappearing in a final outbreak of managerial bossiness, says no. Once again she tries to set her Lord's agenda for him, discouraging Jesus from having the stone moved because she is sure there will be a smell, and at that moment it seems to her more important to save Jesus from the smell than anything else. Once more she thinks she is respecting him by telling him what she thinks he should do, being the grand personage he is, and once more she becomes an obstruction in the path of his purpose by pressing her will on him rather than accepting his. "But Lord, by this time there's a bad odor, for he has been there four days. The body will be decomposing," says Martha, "so don't do it." That statement is what I had in mind when I said earlier that Martha obstructs Jesus.

Martha doesn't at that moment take seriously her own dream that Jesus might bring her brother back to life, and because of the smell she thinks it best that the stone remain where it is. Of course, if the stone remains where it is, there will be no possibility of Lazarus getting out. At this moment Martha's faith is showing its limits. Martha, without realizing it, is hindering what Jesus plans to do. This is to be a miracle—a great, public miracle—a challenging miracle that Jesus is resolved to perform before many witnesses, to demonstrate who he is—the one who is himself the Resurrection and the Life. So Jesus all but ignores Martha's obstructionism. He says, "Did I not tell you that if you believed, you would see the glory of God?" (Jn 11:40). That phrase, "the glory of God," means God on display one way or another, God's power, God's greatness, God's wisdom, God's mercy and God's majesty being shown in action. And that's exactly what they all saw. They took away the stone at Jesus' command, and Lazarus came out alive. Jesus knew what he was doing.

Martha didn't intend to be an obstructionist, but she was. The problem was that her instincts for taking over and being in charge and deciding what was and was not the best thing to do were driving her. Because of this she was not allowing her true faith to teach her submission to Jesus' wisdom and Jesus' power. You and I can learn from her. Trust is wisdom. Our Lord, our Savior, knows what he is doing with our lives. We must not try to control him when he's in action. We must overcome our mistrust of him. I say mistrust because your heart, like my heart, still has sin and unbelief prowling around inside it, and every now and then the instinct of unbelief will try to lead us to hold out on our Lord. Ever since the Garden of Eden unbelief of what God says—the original sin from which what we call original sin took its rise—has opened the door to further sins of every kind. We've got to learn to recognize unbelief for the monstrous anti-God gesture that it is and to say no to it when we find ourselves drawn to any form of noncompliance with any divine word. We cannot doubt that Martha realized afterward how foolish and faithless she had been to try to stop Jesus from having the stone rolled away.

You and I have also had experiences in which, through timidity and mistrust, we shrank back from letting our Lord Jesus have his way without qualification in our lives, and we've learned by experience that that is not the fruitful path to tread. We can be sure that we're going to face further situations in which we'll be tempted to shrink back in just the same way. Let the example of Martha teach us the perversity of doing this when our hand is in Christ's hand, and he, our Savior and our Master, is leading us home through this world to glory.

Martha's Honor

But there is one more event in Martha's life that we must take note of. We've looked at Martha manipulating Jesus (or trying to). We've looked at Martha obstructing Jesus—though without fully realizing what she was doing. Now in the very last glimpse that we have of Martha, the devoted disciple, what we see is Martha truly honoring Jesus. She honors Jesus, and he accepts the honor. In doing that he honors Martha. It's as if Jesus says, "Martha, you're doing it right. You're doing well." The story is in the first three verses of John 12, following straight on from the raising of Lazarus. We read as follows:

> Six days before the Passover, Jesus arrived at Bethany, where Lazarus lived, whom Jesus had raised from the dead. Here a dinner was given in Jesus' honor. Martha served [the meal], while Lazarus was among those reclining at table with him. [Brother Lazarus, in other words, was treated as one of the honored guests.] Then Mary took about a pint of pure nard, an expensive perfume; she poured it on Jesus' feet and wiped his feet with her hair. And the house was filled with the fragrance of the perfume.

We see two things here. One is that Martha served the meal at her home. She's still the hostess, and she's managing this celebration dinner in Jesus' honor. Thus by her service she exalts him, as now she wants to do more than she wants anything else. The second thing is that when Mary makes an extravagant gesture of adoration to the Lord, whom she loves so deeply, Martha doesn't say a word. Martha accepts that Mary has a right to express her worship of Jesus in her own way, and that it's not for Martha to put Mary down by saying, "Oh, you shouldn't do that." Judas in effect said as much (see Jn 12:4–6): "Oh how silly. All this perfume just poured out when it might have been sold for good money. What a waste!" But that's Judas. Mary is doing this because she loves Jesus, which is something Judas knows nothing about. And as I said, Martha offers no criticism. She understands. Martha has learned not to be negative about the devotion of others. She leaves Mary free to honor the Lord in her way—just as Martha is honoring the Lord by organizing this dinner party for him. Here then is Martha honoring Jesus. She is a better, wiser disciple now than when we first met her.

To prepare and serve the meal was, as before, backstage ministry. Martha had to spend hours in the kitchen making the dinner happen. But she doesn't lose her temper this time. She knows what she ought to be doing, and she does it. And Jesus values Martha's ministry as much on this occasion as he did on the earlier occasion before she let herself down.

From Martha's experience with Jesus we may learn that Jesus values all of our backstage ministry that few if any notice, and nobody thanks us for. Perhaps we are tempted sometimes to lose patience because we invest a great deal of ourselves in serving others, and nobody seems to care. The proper way to handle that feeling is to say, "But Jesus knows and Jesus cares." And indeed he does. When we serve others for his sake, we serve him truly, as did Martha at this banquet.

Some of us, like Martha, with the best will in the world, find it very hard not to be bossy and pushy, as she naturally was, jumping to the conclusion that what we think best has to be what God wants too and so not distinguishing our will from his. This unrecognized self-centeredness and pride disfigures our discipleship and makes us from time to time a burden to our families and friends. But Jesus, as we see, led Martha beyond it, and that gives us hope that he can and will do the same for us too. Praise his name!

O Lord our God, we bow before you to confess our need of the same forbearance and mercy that we see in Jesus your Son as he overcomes self-will in his servant Martha. We recognize in ourselves the same habits of treating personal ideas as precepts and priorities for everyone else, and the same willfulness in trying to manage and manipulate other people to make them go our way, and the same real irreverence in trying to bend you to our will so that ours rather than yours is done. We need more self-knowledge and more self-distrust and more humility in our hearts and more dependence on your wisdom in our behavior, and we ask for these good gifts now; in the name of Jesus Christ our Lord. Amen.

Study

1. Who is one of your favorite "Marthas" in your life? What do you appreciate in that person?

2. Review the section "Martha Manipulating Jesus" (pp. 96-100). What do each of Martha's three complaints suggest about her need to grow in discipleship?

3. How does Jesus use each complaint to guide Martha toward being a better disciple?

4. Read John 11:1–44. What scenes from this story stand out in your mind?

5. Verses 5 and 6 say, "Jesus loved Martha and her sister and Lazarus. Yet when he heard that Lazarus was sick, he stayed where he was two more days." Why do you think Jesus did that?

6. Focus on verses 17–27. What steps led Martha to her statement of faith in verse 28?

7. Slowly and thoughtfully read the faith statement of verses 25–26. In what particular situations do these words bring you hope?

8. Read John 12:1–3. What expressions of discipleship to Jesus do you see here?

As you observe the way each of the three siblings expressed their devotion to Jesus in these verses, which is closest to your own natural expression? How?

9. Briefly review the section "Mary and Martha by Turn" (pp. 101-2). Would you say that in your discipleship of Jesus you are more like Martha or more like Mary? Explain.

10. "We all have to learn . . . to be Mary and Martha by turn." What steps could you take to develop better discipleship in your weaker area?

Pray

■ Talk to God about the Mary and Martha qualities in your patterns of serving him. Ask him to search your heart, affirming the strengths in your discipleship and revealing the weaknesses. Then admit those weaknesses to him. Invite God to strengthen you in those weak areas—then commit yourself to doing the work.

■ In God's presence examine your motives for specific acts of service. Are you really looking for recognition and reward? Are you, like Martha, frustrated when people do not take note of your hard work? (Or have you failed to express appreciation for the work of others?) Ask God to purify your motives. Acknowledge that your Lord sees and your Lord cares—regardless of the response of others.

■ Consider taking on a particular task not likely to gain human recognition. As a spiritual discipline perform this to the best of your ability—as a service to God.

■ Meditate on each phrase of Christ's declaration and Martha's confession in John 11:25–26. Use each phrase as a launch for your own prayer on that subject.

Write

John 11 is a vivid account of death. Write your own reflections about death. You could recount the events of the death of someone you love—or your fears of that death at some future time. Use words to shape the pictures in your mind of what happened or might happen. Be honest as you face your grief and your fears. But also write your reflections on God's presence and comfort during that time.

At the end of your journal writing, copy the words of Jesus in John 11:25. Then write your answer to his question.

6

HOPE WHEN I FIND IT HARD TO BELIEVE

Thomas

JOHN 20:19–31

THOMAS SAID, "UNLESS I SEE THE NAIL MARKS IN HIS HANDS and put my finger where the nails were, and put my hand into his side, I will not believe it." Believe what? "Believe that you" (and he's speaking to the other ten disciples out of the original twelve) "have seen the Lord the way you told me you have." What an extraordinary way for Thomas to behave—don't you think? What was going on? Let us inquire.

This was the evening of the day that changed the world quite literally—the day when Jesus who had died as a sacrifice for our sins rose from the dead and showed himself alive and well again on planet Earth. It had been a most momentous evening for the disciples. They'd been huddled behind locked doors, and the reason why the doors were locked is that they were scared of the Jews. The Jewish leaders had recently disposed of their Master, and now the disciples were afraid that the same people would be after them, so they locked the door. That very fact tells you that they were scared, that they were folk without any hope for the future except to keep their heads down and try to escape notice. They certainly weren't anywhere near the joy of knowing that Jesus was risen from the dead and had brought them into newness of life.

Oh yes, the tomb had been found empty earlier that morning, but it was women who had found it so—and it wasn't the way of first-century Jewish men to take too seriously things that women told them. So even though they verified from Peter and John who went there that the tomb really was empty, and even though Mary Magdalene had come to them saying, "I saw the Lord. I really did. I thought it was the gardener, but he spoke to me so I knew it was him," they weren't convinced. So now they were huddled behind locked doors trying to keep each other's spirits up. They were men to be pitied, for they were running scared.

Joy Through a Locked Door

And then through the locked door somehow (they never knew how) came the risen Jesus in his resurrection body. After his rising he could do that kind of thing, namely, appear and then disappear and then appear somewhere else. There are a number of accounts of the risen Lord doing this. This is one of them. Suddenly Jesus was there, standing in the midst.

He spoke, and his first words were "Peace be with you." In those days this was just as casual a greeting as when we wave at someone across the street and say, "Hi." But when Jesus on this occasion said, "Peace be with you," he meant a lot, and I think he spoke the words slowly so that the disciples would think about their meaning.

Peace (Hebrew, *shalom*; Greek, *eirene*) is one of the great Bible words in both Testaments. Its overtones are always of total well-being and happiness, so that *peace* in English is hardly forceful enough to express it. It means, to start with, peace with God, sin forgiven, guilt gone, your person accepted. It also means peace with yourself. If God has forgiven you the grisly things you've done, then you'd better start forgiving yourself; you must learn to be at peace with yourself now that you're at peace with God. It means peace with your circumstances too. If God, the Lord of circumstances, is at peace with you, you can be sure that henceforth he orders and controls circumstances for your good, as Romans 8:28 explicitly declares he does. So even though things may feel rough, just because you know they're there for your good, you can live at peace with them and at peace under them.

"Peace be with you," said Jesus. "Peace with God, peace with yourself, peace with your circumstances. I bring you peace." And when he said this, we're told, he showed them his hands and his side. He didn't do that to identify himself, for they already knew who he was. He did it so that they would see the wounds and the nail prints in his hands and the spear wound in his side and be reminded of what he'd suffered on the cross in order to make for them the peace that he was now bringing to them.

The disciples, we're told, were overjoyed when they saw the Lord among them. But then Jesus repeated his greeting: "Peace be with you." The very fact that he repeated it shows that it was more than a mere greeting. Repetition in Scripture, as in daily life, is for emphasis and to enforce significant meaning. It was supremely important to Jesus that the disciples should understand all that he meant when he said to them, "Peace be with you."

A New Job

Then he went on to commission them. They were to be his

agents and his messengers in the world from that point on. "As the Father has sent me, I am sending you," he said (Jn 20:21). His meaning was: "My Father sent me to bring in and preach the kingdom, and I am sending you to preach the kingdom that I brought in as the focus of the good news about me. I commission you in my role as the King of the kingdom, who died to make peace, and who's risen to bring peace, and who is here with you bringing peace into your own hearts right now. As the Father has been with me in my preaching of the kingdom, so I will be with you as you preach the kingdom, and I will come to those who turn to me anywhere and everywhere, and be with them always. Your message of the kingdom is thus to be a message that focuses on me and brings people to me and thus transforms their lives."

Then came an odd gesture. He breathed on them. He blew breath over them just as you blow breath over the candles of your birthday cake when you're blowing them out. It was a gesture that meant something; it was an acted prophecy of what was to happen at Pentecost. "Receive the Holy Spirit," he said. Those words were a promise: "You are very soon to receive the Holy Spirit."

Then he added, "If you forgive anyone his sins, they are forgiven; and if you do not forgive them, they are not forgiven" (Jn 20:23). What Jesus meant by that was not any kind of priestly prerogative to give or withhold forgiveness for sin at one's discretion. What he's talking about is the gift of discernment. "When the Spirit has come to you," he's saying, "you'll be able to see who of those who say that they've repented and turned from their sin are really genuine. And you'll then be entitled to assure them that because of what I've done on the cross, they're truly forgiven. Equally you'll be able to see who of those who go through the motions and profess to have turned from sin are not genuine but are just hypocrites. And you will then be entitled to tell them what you must in faithfulness tell them: that you see they are not genuine and their sins are not forgiven as yet, since they're not yet real believers."

That this is what is meant seems clear from the disciples' subsequent practice. We see them declaring forgiveness of sins as early as the day of Pentecost, when Peter told his listeners that they must repent and be baptized in the name of Jesus Christ, that is, Jesus recognized as Messiah (with, no doubt, public confession of sins and public profession of repentance as in John's baptism earlier on). Their baptism would declare their personal commitment to the risen Lord. As they did this, so Peter assured them, their sins would be forgiven and they would receive the Holy Spirit (Acts 2:38). And later Peter informs Simon the Sorcerer (I quote the high-flown language of the KJV): "I perceive that thou art still in the gall of bitterness, and in the bond of iniquity." The NIV says: "I see that you are . . . captive to sin" (Acts 8:23). In paraphrase Peter's meaning is: "I can tell that you haven't really repented of your sin, and you haven't really trusted Christ, and you haven't really been born again. You're not a Christian yet, so your sin is not forgiven yet." The promised remitting and retaining of sins is a matter of declaration, based on discernment.

What Thomas Missed

All of this happened while Thomas wasn't there. You can see that for the ten it was the most momentous thing imaginable. They had been in the depths of despair and fear and hopelessness. Jesus had come and brought light into their darkness, set them on their feet again, commissioned them, given them a future, given them a task, given them a promise of his enabling for the task, the gift of the Spirit—no less. Can you wonder then that they were just bubbling over when Thomas turned up? In he comes, and they tell him all about it. "We have seen the Lord!" they shout (Jn 21:25). And Thomas folds his arms and acts cool. He simply brushes it off, shakes his head and says to them, "Unless I see the nail marks in his hands and put my finger where the nails were, and put my hand into his side, I will not believe it." What was going on in his mind to make him react like that?

Certainly his nonbelief boomeranged on himself. By taking this line Thomas sentenced himself to another week of hopelessness, while his ten friends were rejoicing in the knowledge that Jesus was alive. But Thomas chose not to believe it. So he had a further week of misery and gloom that, if his attitude had been different, he might have avoided. We often speak of him as "doubting Thomas." I'm not saying that it is absolutely unfitting to call him that, but I would rather call him Thomas the Skeptic. Skeptics allege weakness in other people's reasoning and withhold assent from their conclusions. That is precisely what Thomas did in this case.

The Perils of Skepticism

Skepticism is never an attitude that calls for admiration. Skepticism always has something willful about it. We meet two sorts of doubters in this world. There are the people who would like to be Christians but can't bring themselves to the point of commitment. They are the woeful doubters who by their own confession wish they could believe. I think it is possible to do something for people who really feel that way. They say they have a problem. Well, let's see what the problem is. Those who understand the Christian faith in its biblical expression know that it has no internal inconsistencies and that all sober reason and all factual knowledge and evidence is for it rather than against it. If the doubter's problem is an honest one, through honest reasoning it can be overcome.

But in Thomas's case I don't think we are looking at woeful doubt at all. I think what we see is willful doubting or willed skepticism. Thomas has made up his mind that he isn't going to believe, and his reasons for doing so, though very human and fully understandable, are not really admirable because they are not really rational. Here is what I think was going on inside him.

Thomas the Melancholic

I ask again the question that opened this chapter: What led Thomas to behave as he did? Four factors, I believe, were operating. I think, first, that temperament had something to do with it. I suspect that Thomas was one of those folk whom we call (or our grandparents used to call) *melancholics*. These are the people called depressives now. When I say this, I am not thinking of persons in pathological and clinical depression, whom medication and psychiatry can help, but of the temperamental depressives that in my youth we called dismal Jimmies, the Eeyores and Puddleglums of the human race. Their minds are anchored in gloom and despondency. They live on the edge of despair, every now and then toppling over the edge right into it. This comes to them naturally, so naturally that they can't bring themselves to doubt that their black thinking is realistic and right. They see themselves as the ones—the discerning ones, the only ones—who really know how life really is. Nothing is right for them unless something's wrong. All good news is really too good to be true. Their attitude is comic in a way, but tragic for them because in their self-indulgence (for that is what it actually is) they yield to their gloomy temperament very quickly and so get trapped in the negativity that such a temperament generates. When we allow our temperament to get on top of us and control us, it really is a sort of self-indulgence. Among aspects of our fallen nature that we must learn to deny is the lure of our temperament.

It isn't only melancholy folks who need to learn this discipline. There are the sanguine folks who are always happy-go-lucky and overly optimistic. If they're ever going to become realists, they've got to learn not to indulge their temperament. There are phlegmatic people who are always cool as a cucumber, detached and casual, even when they need to be warm and excited. At such times they too need to deny their temperament and seek to warm up. There are the choleric characters who are always restless and wanting change, and who again and again have to deny their temperament and practice patience. These are examples of what I mean. Our temperament can lead us astray and victimize us one way or another, and I cannot help wondering whether you and I have as yet seriously come to terms with our temperament.

I type Thomas as one of the melancholics, the gloomy ones. Why do I do that? Well, John has already told us that when Jesus broke the news of Lazarus' death to the disciples and said to them, "Our friend Lazarus . . . is dead . . . let us go to him," Thomas commented. "Let us also go that we may die with him." Whether "him" is Lazarus or Jesus (you can make a case for either), Thomas's remark seems to reveal a gloomy temperament quite devastated by the knowledge of Lazarus's death and now feeling that everything now was and would continue to be as bad as it could possibly be.

And so when his friends tell him on the first Easter evening that Jesus has appeared to them risen and alive, so that the tragedy of Calvary is now swallowed up in the triumph of resurrection, Thomas's heart said, *Oh no, it's these wretched optimists again. You can't take a thing they say seriously.* People with a melancholy temperament, as I pointed out above, tend to believe they are much more realistic about things than folk who are not moody and despairing in the way that they themselves are. This somberness of temperament, with its melancholy sense of foreboding, was operating in Thomas to make him unreasonably skeptical. It had been Thomas's habit all his life, I guess, to indulge his temperament rather than rationally challenge the negative conclusions to which it regularly jumped, and at this moment he became the victim of it in a very direct way. His wild words were from this standpoint an unthought-out expression of the spirit of disillusionment, gloom and pessimism with which, so he felt (and had been feeling all his life), true wisdom will always lie.

Thomas the Stressed

Then, second, I think stress had something to do with his attitude. He had lived three days of appalling strain (as had all the disciples). Just think of it. The previous week Thomas had been part of the triumphal entry into Jerusalem, with Jesus riding on a donkey and fulfilling the prophecy that this was the way that Jerusalem's king was to come into the city (see Zech 9:9). Crowds had cheered and shouted, "Blessed is he who comes in the name of the Lord, Hosanna to the son of David." They had thrown palm branches into the road as a sort of welcome carpet for Jesus' donkey to walk on. It had been a tremendous, triumphant moment, and the disciples had been sure that now somehow Jesus was going to proclaim himself king. They had come to

Jerusalem with the Messiah fully in control, as they thought, and their hearts were high.

Then had come the days of conflict in the temple, with Jesus deliberately challenging, even baiting, the scribes and the Pharisees and Sadducees, the official rulers of religion. Next had come the arrest and the show trial—that travesty of justice, as everyone concerned knew perfectly well it was. Then the disciples had heard the crowd yelling, "Crucify Jesus. Give us Barabbas. We'd rather have Barabbas." And they had seen Jesus rushed out to Calvary—Skull Hill, as it was called—and nailed to the cross, in the cruel execution process of crucifixion.

Can you imagine what it was like to go through those days? *Harrowing* must be a weak word for the disciples' descent from supreme joy and excitement to what seemed absolute tragedy and disaster. Watching a crucifixion would bring the most hardhearted to tears. It is a terribly cruel death. And this was the death of Jesus their Lord. They were all there, for sure. They saw his agony as his lifeblood ebbed away. They heard his words from the cross. Did they understand them as the majestic words of ministry and testimony and victory that they were? I doubt they did. By the time the body was taken down from the cross, they had been through an awful lot. They were utterly crushed and totally at a loss. Thomas had been with them throughout, and Thomas (because of his temperament, I imagine) made heavier weather of it than the rest of them. Perhaps the reason why Thomas was not with the ten when Jesus came was that he had gotten beyond the point where he could enjoy being with anyone and was spending long periods on his own.

Now what his friends are saying to him (possibly with slapping on the back and the like) comes through to him like this: "Cheer up, Thomas. Everything in the garden is lovely after all. He's risen. We've seen him. It's all wonderful. Whoopee!" And Thomas's emotionally exhausted heart says, *I can't take any more. Whether they're right or wrong, this is just too much to cope with.* I think he deliberately pushed away from himself the stunning news about Jesus because he was, as we say, utterly stressed out and totally numb inside. He'd gone from highest hope to deepest despair. Now they're telling him to return from deepest despair to highest hope again—and he simply doesn't feel he's got what it takes to do it. His wild words were from this standpoint a distancing of himself from the entire issue of whether Jesus, whose dreadful, degrading death had broken Thomas's heart, was alive again or not.

I don't think Thomas could justify his attitude, but I think we can all of us understand it. Surely we've all of us been through times of strain and upheaval that have brought us to the point where we feel, *I can't take anymore of anything. Just keep quiet and go away.* I think this is part of what Thomas's reply to his friends was expressing. Soldiers who have been through war sometimes end up inwardly numb as far as joy and hope and excitement are concerned. They have become, in T. S. Eliot's phrase, "hollow men." It is as if their power to feel positively about anything has been destroyed by the strain and pressure of things they endured during the hostilities. The description that fits them comes again from T. S. Eliot: "living—and partly living." There are lots of people like that, and I think they are all mirrored in Thomas. He's had a week of appalling stress. His temperament is against him as we have seen, and now the strain of events on top of his temperament makes it impossible for him, so he feels, to take seriously any word of hope—or any bit of good news at all. Inside, as was stated above, he is saying, *Here's another shock; I'm almost round the bend as it is; I can't handle it;*

I'm staying switched off; just leave me alone. It's not a rational attitude but a very human one. I think we can and should sympathize.

You who read this may be a person who, perhaps because your temperament is a bit like Thomas's, perhaps because you too have had harrowing experiences that have numbed you inside, cannot embrace the good news of a Savior who died to win peace for you and has risen to bring new life and joy to you. Your heart says, *I like a bit of religion; it soothes my spirit. But don't ask me actually to believe anything as hopeful and marvelous as what Christians believe about Jesus. I just can't handle that.* Strain produces that sort of reaction, and I think strain had much to do with Thomas's unresponsiveness to the other disciples.

Thomas the Prideful

Then there's a third thing. I think that pride had something to do with Thomas's skepticism. John's Gospel seems to hint that Thomas wasn't the world's brightest guy. He was slow on the uptake, and I think he felt it. Most of us have been through moments when we've had to say to ourselves, *Oh, boy. I wasn't very smart there, was I.* I guess Thomas was well acquainted with that feeling. He was a twin. We're not told that his brother or sister was smarter than he, but it might have been so. Twins often have a close rapport with each other, so if he was the less bright one, he would have a constant awareness of the comparison, and it would have added to his burden. To feel inferior all the time is hurtful, to say the least.

John records at least one occasion when Thomas blurted out a rather thick-witted remark. Jesus had just spoken tremendous words of comfort and joy: "Do not let your hearts be troubled.

Trust in God; trust also in me. In my Father's house are many rooms. . . . I am going there to prepare a place for you. And if I go and prepare a place for you, I will come back and take you to be with me that you also may be where I am" (Jn 14:1–3). That's a marvelous promise, you will agree, and its thrust seems plain.

Then Jesus said, "You know the way to the place where I am going." And Thomas piped up, "Lord, we don't know where you are going, so how can we know the way?" (See Jn 14:4–5.) This was, I think, Thomas being himself—slow on the uptake. Thomas is an honest fellow, and he admits that he hasn't a clue what Jesus is talking about.

I suspect that John in writing his Gospel put in this detail so that we would be prepared later in the story to find Thomas behaving in the way of a man who is slow and feels slow and tries to compensate for it by acting super smart. We know how a person who feels a little bit left behind, a little bit thick in comparison with others, will behave. If we actually are that person, we know how we ourselves behave. We attempt something the psychologists call compensation. We deliberately try to act smart to cover the fact that inside we know we aren't smart. Our minds go into reflex action that is meant to keep our end up and banish any sense of having been made rings around and put down. Here, I think, we see Thomas trying to act very shrewd and very hardheaded. Thomas says to his friends in effect, "Now wait a minute. You're telling me you saw Jesus. All right, that's what you say. But we need solid evidence; at least I do. You didn't touch him, did you? Haven't you ever heard of people who've seen visions and there wasn't anything really there? If I'd been with you, I would have insisted on touching him. You can be mistaken about things you think you see. You don't make the same sort of mistakes though if you actually touch a person. But you didn't touch him, did you? You didn't think of touching him, did you? You guys—you're not so smart." That's what Thomas's wild words seem to be telling them.

Then he says, "I won't believe until I have touched him. I won't believe until I've got sufficient evidence. I am asking for more proof than you asked for. I'm not going to be taken in, as I'm afraid you guys have been." It's pathetic, I know, but I think that's the direct meaning of what Thomas said. And it was pride, the wounded pride of his bruised ego, victim of a thousand put-downs, that led him to take this line.

Perhaps this is being read by someone who is willfully skeptical about the resurrection of Jesus, not because you think the evidence for it is intrinsically insufficient (it has in the past been described as the best attested fact in history) but because you are trying to prove to some Christian friend that you are a bit smarter than they are. So you tell them that they believe for insufficient reasons, and you ask for more evidence than they can produce. And you're doing that really in order to try to put balm on your own deflated ego. You are trying to compensate for the feeling that you are not too smart. So you're going to act super intelligent. The name for your attitude is pride—pride of heart and of intellect. As I said, pride seems to have had something to do with Thomas's attitude. And pride, I know, has something to do with the skepticism of some folks today.

Thomas the Resentful

Then there's a fourth factor that may have been part of the story. Resentment might have had something to do with Thomas's reaction of unbelief. Thomas could have been expressing his resentment of the fact that Jesus had come to the ten and hadn't come to him. They had received a blessing that he himself had missed, and he resented that whole situation and his rejection of what his friends were saying was a way of expressing that resentment. There are folks today who have seen others blessed, and they resent the blessings that those others enjoy. They resent the smile on the face of the man or the woman who can say, "I'm a Christian, and I've found in Christ the secret of new life." They haven't found it themselves, and they resent the fact that others have found it. They themselves are still in the toils, making heavy weather of life, and here's someone who says, "I have peace. I have joy. I love Jesus. It's a new life. Everything's wonderful." And they resent that because of their own hurts inside. Resentment along with a gloomy temperament, emotional exhaustion and a passion to act clever may very well have contributed to Thomas's negative attitude and prompted his wild words.

Some people make a hero of Thomas—as if his hardheadedness and skepticism were something to admire. Really, as I urged earlier, it's not an attitude to admire at all. It wasn't wisdom; it wasn't virtue; it wasn't reasonable behavior. It was, as I have just said, a sad case of a man with a temperament that he hadn't come to terms with, and the shock of disappointment still on his soul, feeling he has to keep his end up by acting smart, all the while burning with resentment that anybody could be blessed in a way that he hadn't experienced himself. The result of his skepticism, as we saw, is that he sentenced himself to a very black week. I don't suppose that during that week the ten others and Thomas said much to each other at all.

Thomas and Jesus

Seven days later, however, Jesus appears once more, and once more utters his glorious greeting, "Peace be with you." Then he speaks directly to Thomas. Strikingly, what he says isn't a word of rebuke for Thomas's skepticism or irreverence. There was something really irreverent, as well as really gruesome, about Thomas's insistence, "I want to finger the nail prints. I want to put my hand into the spear wound that made such a mess of his side," but Jesus, although he knows perfectly well what Thomas had said, does not criticize or chide him for it. He says simply (I paraphrase Jn 20:27), "Thomas, put out your finger. I want you to touch me. See my hands? You wanted to feel the wounds? Well, feel them. Put your finger here and run it over the nail prints, and then reach out your hand and put it into this hole in my side. Don't be a doubter, stop being a skeptic, and believe, as your fellow disciples already do."

Jesus was gentle with Thomas. I think the Savior's kindness with him was marvelous. We need to remember that Thomas was one of the twelve whom Jesus chose, fully knowing their strengths, weaknesses, talents and limitations, to prepare and equip for the worldwide church-founding tasks that would follow his ascension. Jesus had loved and valued Thomas from the start and was dealing with him now as one being groomed for special ministry. The Savior's way, however, of helping Thomas to assurance about the ongoing reality of his resurrection life is a model of how today he works in the lives of many coming to faith out of total spiritual darkness, and it is from this point of view that we are reviewing it. And as was noted above, what we see in Jesus' ministry to Thomas is quite simply overwhelming kindness. Thomas had painted himself into a corner, and Jesus affirms him by taking him at his word, meeting him where he is and saying in effect, "If it is going to help you to finger the wounds in my body, then finger them. Only stop acting the unbeliever, Thomas. Acknowledge the reality of my rising. Believe."

We're not told whether Thomas actually did what Jesus was inviting him to do. Maybe he stood, bowed, even knelt; we don't know. What is apparent, though, is that Thomas was absolutely broken. "My Lord, and my God," he said. And in saying that, he made the perfect confession of faith, the fullest and clearest that is found anywhere in the Gospels. It is as if he said, "Lord Jesus, yes I believe. I believe that you are alive from the dead, and I should have believed that a week ago, and I honor you now, both for your glorious rising and for your loving ministry to me at this moment. You are God and I should be your person, your servant, your worshiper from now on. And whatever you send in your providence, your ordering of things, I should take as from your hand, and I should recognize that henceforth I'll never be out of your sight but shall always be in your fellowship. I didn't believe that before, but I believe it now."

Thomas's confession went on to say in effect, "Jesus, you are God, my Lord and my God. Forgive me, Lord, for my skepticism and my irreverence. Now I take you afresh as all that you are, my Lord and my God, Author of my being, Savior of my soul. And I know that when I take you as mine, you take me as yours, and thus the covenant is established and confirmed. As in marriage, so here: vows confirm a permanent commitment. Here and now I vow to be yours, Lord. You are my Lord and my God."

Jesus responded by speaking the last and in one way the most wonderful of all the beatitudes. What makes it the most wonderful? The fact that it leads us into the life and enjoyment of the rest of the beatitudes, which without Thomas-like faith you and I will never know. "Thomas, because you have seen you have believed," said Jesus. Now comes the beatitude, the statement of blessing, "Blessed are all those who have not seen but yet have believed."

Believing the Witnesses

This is a beatitude for you and me. In the providence of God we weren't set to live in the early years of the first century A.D., and so we didn't and couldn't see Jesus with our bodily eyes. There are people who say, "Oh if I could have been in Palestine and watched Jesus; if I could have been at the tomb and seen him rise, I would certainly believe." I don't think so. If that were really true, you would be believing now on the testimony of those who did see and gave their lives for the witness that they bore to the Christ whom they saw. There's every reason to believe. The original disciples bore witness. They preached the gospel, brought persons of many nationalities to faith, founded churches and wrote material that now serves to guide all of us in later generations into faith like theirs. There's no reason whatsoever to follow speculative skeptical scholarship and doubt the New Testament witness to Jesus—those who wrote it, after all, put their lives on the line for it. Most of the apostles were martyred. All of them were willing to die for Christ. If they had had the slightest doubt as to whether the Christ they preached was for real or if there had been the slightest pretense in the attitude they first adopted, they wouldn't have behaved like that. They knew, and so they were prepared to give their lives rather than deny or go back on what they knew. Their testimony has come down the centuries to us. Isn't it adequate?

Just think for a moment about the one fact of the resurrection. Christianity is inexplicable if Jesus didn't rise from the dead. Where then did it come from? How did it start? How should we explain the fact that from the start it was faith with a risen Jesus as its focus? And if Jesus didn't rise from the dead, why didn't the Jews at once produce the body from the grave to show that Jesus wasn't risen and that all this talk about resurrection faith was nonsense? The answer is simple: they didn't produce the body because they couldn't produce the body. The body wasn't there; the grave was empty; Jesus had risen. Isn't the testimony good? Doesn't it make sense? Doesn't it fit together? Isn't it credible?

As I travel around through Canada, the United States, Australia, New Zealand and Britain, I meet people who have never been to Vancouver—where I live. But I tell them that Vancouver exists and is a fine place, and they believe me. They believe about Vancouver on my testimony. They don't assume that I'm some sort of jackal who goes around deceiving people for the fun of it. Why should we accuse the New Testament preachers and writers of being professional deceivers—con men, as we would express it today? Is that a reasonable thing to do?

It would be unreasonable if people refused to believe my declaration that there's such a place as Vancouver just because they've never themselves seen it. It would be equally unreasonable if you and I refused to believe in the resurrection of Jesus and the truth of Christianity just because in the providence of God we didn't live in the first century so that we could see the Savior in the flesh.

Stretching a Hand Toward Jesus

"Blessed," said Jesus, "are those who have not seen and yet have believed." We secondhand believers recognize the trustworthiness of the testimony of those who did see and bore the firsthand witness so that all the world might know what they knew. It's the most reasonable just as it's the most joyful thing in the world to accept the testimony of those who knew and on the basis of their testimony to stretch out your own empty hand of faith toward Jesus and to say to him in echo of Thomas's words: "My Lord and my God! I know you're there. I know you're real. The testimony to you is testimony that no honest man can refuse. I need you, Lord Jesus. I'm in the dark just as Thomas was in the dark. I'm living in the dark of depression, the dark of disappointment, the dark of a play-acting sort of life, acting smart though I know I'm foolish, acting happy though I know I'm miserable, keeping up a front while living behind a mask that I dare not drop. Lord, it hurts, and I'm in the dark because I've been playing these games for so long. And Lord, there is nothing that would bring me more joy than the new life that the gospel promises, the life of pardon and peace and fellowship with you and the life of glory beyond. My Lord, my God, my Jesus, come into my life and give me what you gave Thomas."

John ends this chapter by saying, "These [signs] are written that you may believe that Jesus is the Christ, the Son of God, and that by believing you may have life in his name" (Jn 20:31). John would, I think, approve of what I wrote in the previous paragraph.

I wrote at the beginning that though as a member of the human race I think I can understand and sympathize with Thomas, and though I believe I know how Thomas was thinking—since there have been moments in the past when I've thought in a very similar way—I still cannot justify Thomas's unbelief. You now see why. If there are any Thomases among my readers, I have to tell you that I can't justify your unbelief either. It's willful. It's chosen, not constrained. It's not reasonable. It involves denying cogent testimony. Such denial makes no sense.

God help us all, then, to come to terms with our temperaments, with our experiences of strain, with those proud and really foolish gestures that we make in attempts to show that we're smarter than other people, and with any resentment we feel that others seem to have found a blessing that we haven't found. Coming to terms with those four realities will mean that we recognize that our skepticism is irrational, having its base in our feelings about ourselves and not in anything else. And we shall see too that we cannot justify ourselves in holding back any longer from the commitment to Jesus Christ that Thomas made when he said to him, "My Lord and my God." So by the grace of God may we all be blessed as those who follow Thomas into faith.

Glorious Lord Jesus, we have been reading about you and thinking about you. In all this we have been acknowledging and realizing your presence with us. Jesus, Lord, Master, speak to each of us, just as we need to be spoken to, about our own pains and grief of depression and disappointment and play-acting and resenting the way things are. You delivered Thomas from all these pains and grief, and we ask you to deliver us too. When Thomas said to you, "My Lord and my God," it was the start of a new life for him, and we covet that same new life for ourselves. Lord Jesus, draw us out to speak to you in just the same tones and terms as Thomas finally did, and bring us out of our darkness into your glorious light, setting us free from those things that hold us down in the dark and liberating our spirits to rise into joy and triumph in everlasting fellowship with yourself. Hear us, Lord Jesus, and by your Spirit draw near to us and minister to us as we need to be ministered to. We ask this in your own holy name. Amen.

Study

1. What do you see of yourself in Thomas?

2. Read John 20:19–31. What happened at Jesus' first visit that was important to the disciples (vv. 19–23)?

3. Imagine yourself in Thomas's sandals at the second meeting (vv. 24–29). What changes take place in his thoughts and in his emotions?

4. What is included in Thomas's statement, "My Lord and my God!" (v. 28)?

5. Thomas was dealing with four possible obstacles to his faith: temperament, stress, pride and resentment. When and how has one of these

forces made it hard for you to believe in Jesus?

6. When you have had moments of doubt or skepticism about Christianity, what questions or problems came to your mind?

7. Focus on John 20:30–31. According to these verses what form should our faith take?

8. Review the section titled "Believing the Witnesses" (pp. 129-31). What evidences of Christ's resurrection do you find most convincing?

9. Review the section titled "Stretching a Hand Toward Jesus" (pp. 131-33). When and how have you responded to this invitation? If that has not yet occurred in your life, what steps toward belief are you willing to take now?

10. Thomas said to Jesus, "My Lord and my God." Pray your own prayer expressing to God your own level of faith and commitment.

Pray

The Benedictine Christians of the sixth century introduced a form of meditation and prayer called *lectio divina*. They used a pattern composed of several steps that allowed them to focus on a particular text, to think about it from various angles, to pray and to try to become aware of what God revealed to them through that passage. Use this modified form of the *lectio divina* to absorb the important teachings that Jesus gave to Thomas in John 14:1–7.

Silencio (Silence)

Take time to be silent; prepare to communicate with God as he expresses himself to you in this passage of Scripture. After a period of quiet, ask God's help as you enter this session of meditative prayer.

Lectio (Read)

Read John 14:1–7 aloud several times slowly. Allow its words and meanings to sink into your soul.

Meditatio (Meditate)

Meditation is a little like chewing. It is slow and thorough. Write notes about what you see in this passage. Make connections between the various sections. Ask yourself, "What do these words from God say?" "What do they mean?" Place who you are and what you do next to this passage and ask God to examine you. Continue to write your findings.

Oratio (Prayer)

Pray using the passage as an outline for your prayer. Read the passage phrase-by-phrase, responding to God after each.

Contemplatio (Contemplation)

Wait in stillness once more. Ask that God bring to your mind any areas of your life that you need to shape more closely to his design as revealed in this passage. Contemplate God's love and power as it is revealed here.

Incarnatio (Live it Out)

What precisely ought you to be believing, thinking and doing as a result of this passage? Make notes about how you hope to bring these words from Jesus into your current practice.

Write

Jesus said in John 14:6, "I am the way and the truth and the life. No one comes to the Father except through me." Write of some attempts you have made to find a way, truth or life by some other route. Then write of how Jesus has become the way, truth and life to you.

7

HOPE WHEN I HAVE DONE
SOMETHING TERRIBLE

Simon Peter

JOHN 21; 1 PETER;
2 PETER

IMON SON OF JOHN, *DO YOU TRULY LOVE ME*?" (EMPHASIS
added, see Jn 21:15–17). That was Jesus' searching question for
Simon, and it's an equally searching question for you and me. He
put it to Simon three times in as many minutes. We who claim to
be his disciples today should think of him as putting it to us at
every turn of the road in our life journey. We're now going to
explore the way in which our Lord turned Simon, son of John,
into Peter the rock (Greek, *Petros*), the anchor of the early
church, a flawed human being who yet became able to answer
yes to this question from his Lord.

In Britain there is a proverb: *You can't make a silk purse out
of a sow's ear.* In other words, there's a limit to what you can do
with the material that's available to you. I want to begin our
study of Simon Peter by saying God can indeed make silk purses

out of sow's ears—and he does. That is a wonderful truth. God does amazing things with flawed human material. Even more wonderful is the fact that he uses these flawed folk as he goes along, giving them a significant ministry, even though the transformation isn't yet complete and there's still a long way to go with his reconstruction of their characters. This ought to be good news for you and me who know our souls to be flawed. Let's be honest before the Lord about that. None of us is perfect; all of us are a long way from being perfect. Nonetheless, God is in the process of reconstructing us in the image of our Savior, and he is pleased to use us in his service as the work goes along. Simon Peter is a spectacular example of that twofold truth. That's what we're going to see as we follow his story.

We start with three facts that were there right from the first meeting between Simon and the Savior, the meeting that's recorded in John 1:35–42, when Andrew, Simon's brother, brought him to Jesus.

A Natural Leader

The first fact is that Simon was a natural leader. He ran his own fishing business, and he was the kind of brash, confident, warmhearted, outgoing person who assumes command in every situation, taking for granted that he's the person who ought to be leading, and acting accordingly. As you read the story of Simon in the Gospels, you find him doing this over and over. For instance, look at the occasion at Caesarea Philippi, recorded in Matthew 16:13–19, when Jesus said, "Who do people say the Son of Man is?" After the disciples had replied that different people were saying different things, Jesus came back at them and said, "But . . . who do *you* say I am?" (emphasis added). He was asking all of them, but it was Simon who spoke up and gave their answer. Simon took it for granted that he should be the spokesman for the group when something really important had to be said. Simon said, "You are the Christ, the son of the living God." He was right, of course, and Jesus at once assured him of the God-taught rightness of what he had said by declaring, "Blessed are you, Simon son of John, for this was not revealed to you by man, but by my Father in heaven." The point for us to note, however, is that in thus answering the question on behalf of all the disciples, Simon was acting as leader.

There's another example of the same thing at the end of John 6. Jesus has given some heavy teaching about himself as the Bread of Life, and he's explained that receiving and consuming him as the Bread of Life means eating his flesh and drinking his blood. The listeners have no idea what he's talking about, but they don't like the sound of it. So they leave him. Jesus turns to the disciples and wonders out loud whether they too want to abandon him. Once again it's Simon who speaks up on behalf of the whole group, saying, "Lord, to whom shall we go?" He is speaking for all of them when he says to Jesus, "You have the words of eternal life" (Jn 6:67–68). Once again he's right, and once again we see him taking the lead.

These two episodes not only show Simon acting as leader of the first disciples, they also show something that is crucially important for all of us. Simon here says what you and I must learn to say if ever we are to share the life that Jesus came to bring. Yes, he is the Christ, the God-anointed Savior. And yes, he has the words of eternal life. If you and I would enter into life, we must learn to make Simon's two affirmations our own.

A Spiritual Leader

The second fact is that from the moment Jesus met Simon, he

made it plain that he was casting the fisherman for the role of a spiritual leader. At that first meeting Jesus said to him, "You are Simon, son of John. You will be called 'Cephas' (which, when translated, is Peter)" (Jn 1:42). *Peter* means "the rock." *Cephas* is Aramaic and *Petros* is Greek, and both signify a rock. Then, as now, "rock" was a sort of nickname: rocklike people are sometimes called "Rocky" today, and the nuance was the same when Jesus named Simon "Cephas." "Rocky," says Jesus, "is the name I give you. That's what you're going to be called, because that's what you're going to be." It's a prophetic word. Simon is going to become the "rock man." Jesus is showing that his plan for Simon was that this natural leader should become a spiritual leader as well.

Other things that Jesus said about Simon pointed in the same direction. Think, for instance, of the first miraculous catch of fish (Lk 5:1–11). Jesus had borrowed the fisherman's boat for a teaching session. Simon had taken the boat out a few yards from the shore, and from it Jesus had taught the crowd. After the teaching session was over Jesus said (I paraphrase), "Well now, put out into deep water, let down your nets, catch something." Simon said to him, "Lord, we fished all night before you came along, and we didn't catch anything at all. Still, you tell me to do it, so I'll do it—of course I will." He did it, and I suppose the boat intercepted a shoal of fish. Before he knew where he was, the nets were full. It was such an awesome demonstration of the power of Jesus that Simon, who was a great man for blurting things out, just said what came into his heart at that moment, "Lord, I'm not fit to be in your company when you can do things like this. You should depart from me for I am a sinful man." Clearly what he is expressing is his sense that Jesus is a holy, unique, more-than-human person—in other words, his utter awe in Jesus' presence. But what Jesus said was, "No, no, none of that. Don't be afraid." (Awe at the supernatural regularly produces some fear.) "From now on, Simon, you are going to catch people. You're going to be a fisher of human beings." We can see what a weighty promise that was. It was another indication that Jesus wanted Simon as a spiritual leader, in this case as a pioneer in evangelism.

After Simon had confessed Jesus as Christ and Son of God at Caesarea Philippi, Jesus said to him, "You are Peter, and on this rock I will build my church" (Mt 16:18). "Rock" here is *petra,* not *Petros,* and this verbal variant shows that Jesus wasn't simply saying, "You, Simon, in your own person, are the one on whom I am going to build the church." He would have said and Matthew would have written "on you" or "on this Petros" if he had meant that. No, the rock is the faith that Simon had expressed and that would be the means of making Simon into the man he was going to be.

In any case, Jesus' building of the church wasn't going to be the setting up of any kind of institution with a single head. It was going to be a matter of drawing people to faith in himself through the gospel word that calls us all to faith, and of so uniting them with himself by the Spirit as to create the supernatural fellowship, which is his body. That's church-building according to Jesus. So I think the Roman Catholic understanding of the passage, which sees it as a personal promise to Simon Peter and his successors and as having to do with some form of institutional headship, isn't the natural one. What then did Jesus mean when he told Peter, "I will give you the keys of the kingdom of heaven"? What he meant was, "I'm going to make you into an evangelist, Peter. You're going to preach the gospel, which opens the door into the kingdom for your hearers." Jesus said that in a personal address to Simon, thereby indicating that the promise, which applies to everyone who ever preaches the gospel, was going to be fulfilled to him in a special way. So indeed it was, as we shall see.

Jesus revealed Simon Peter's destiny as a spiritual leader on yet another occasion. This time it was the evening of Jesus' arrest, the day before the Passion. The disciples were together with the Lord at what we call the Last Supper. Jesus had looked ahead to the future, as he was able to do, and said quite specifically to his disciple, "Simon, Simon, Satan has asked to sift you as wheat." *You* is in the plural, meaning all the disciples. Jesus was talking to Simon specifically, but he was talking about them all. This "sifting like wheat" is a reference to the way in which farmers used to winnow the grain in ancient Palestine. First they would beat it out on their threshing floor, separating the husks from the wheat inside them. Then they would throw everything into the air with a fork or a big shovel, and the wind would blow away the chaff (the husks), leaving them with the wheat on their threshing floor. What had landed was wheat without husks, with the chaff sifted out. Jesus was telling Simon that the disciples were going to be (as we used to say back in Britain) put through the wringer, treated, that is, in a rough and harrowing way to see what they were made of. But then he continued, "I have prayed for you, Simon"—singular now, just Simon—"that your faith may not fail. And when you have turned back, strengthen your brothers" (Lk 22:31). Jesus knows that after the rough time that faced Simon, the former fisherman would turn back to minister support and strength to his fellow disciples. This was a further indication of the leadership role that Jesus has in mind for Simon Peter.

From these events we can see that Jesus, right from the start, wanted Simon as a spiritual leader and sought to prepare him for the role. There is nothing strange about this. Jesus still from time to time puts his hand on people for spiritual leadership quite early in their pilgrimage. It happens—and it constitutes a calling that those who receive it know they have got to accept.

A Loyal Follower

And now a third fact about Simon Peter, which also is clear from the Gospel story. From the time that he first met Jesus standing by the Lake of Gennesaret, he was loyal to him as his own true leader. Whether at first he understood all that was involved in being one of Jesus' followers, we may doubt. But Simon knew that this was the person in whose hands he should rest his destiny, whom he should follow and obey. At point after point in the story we see Simon trying to live out this commitment. So he professed special personal loyalty to his Lord after the Last Supper. When Jesus told the disciples, "This very night you will all fall away on account of me, for it is written, 'I will strike the shepherd and the sheep of the flock will be scattered,' " Simon immediately said, " 'Even if all fall away on account of you, I never will.' 'I tell you the truth,' Jesus answered, 'This very night, before the cock crows, you will disown me three times.' But Simon declared, 'Even if I have to die with you, I will never disown you' " (Mt 26:31-35). And he really believed what he said.

You can see that Simon Peter thought of himself as totally committed to Jesus his leader. Like the other disciples, he was a believer before the cross. He didn't understand all that was planned for Jesus or all that Jesus said. You would have to say that he was a beginner believer. But in terms of having bound himself absolutely to be Jesus' follower in life and death, his commitment was a reality. As honestly as he knows, Simon has made it and intends to stick by it.

We know, as the story goes on to show, that there was a great

deal of pride and self-confidence in Simon, and much self-igno-
rance and real weakness were hiding behind that pride and self-
confidence. But that doesn't alter the fact that Simon, son of
John, saw himself as completely committed to Jesus. So these
are the three basic facts that we must bear in mind in Simon's
story. He was a natural leader, Jesus called him to be a spiritual
leader, and Simon Peter was committed to his Lord.

Loyalty with Frailty

The story of Simon Peter prior to the cross unfolds as a tale of
foolishness and finally of failure. He wasn't up to the demands of
his discipleship, and this is what the story shows most clearly.
Jesus was patient with him; Jesus actually used him, as he used
the other disciples, in preaching ministry. At one point Jesus
sent the disciples out as an advance preaching party to let folk
know that he was coming. Scripture says that they preached the
kingdom and they healed. Jesus gave these raw and unfinished
disciples this role in the work of the kingdom. It really happened.
But that doesn't alter the fact that the Simon of these three years
of discipleship was a Simon who constantly spoke in a way that
was thoughtless and silly, and who sometimes did things that
were thoughtless and silly. We speak of Simon as suffering from
foot-in-mouth disease because again and again when he opened
his mouth, he put his foot in it. He said things that would have
been better not said, just as he did things that would have been
better not done.

For instance, Simon is out in the boat with the disciples and a
storm has come up. They're rowing hard, wondering whether
they're ever going to make it to the other side of the lake, and
Jesus comes to them walking on the water. Jesus says, "Don't be
frightened. It's me." And Simon says (ask yourself why), "Lord,

if it's really you, tell me to come to you on the water." Why did
he want the experience of walking on water? What was in his
mind? It's hard to guess, unless it was sheer bravado; but in any
case, in retrospect I think he would have been the first to admit
it was a rather silly thing to say. Mind you, Jesus took him at his
word and said, "If that's what you want, come." So he came, and
just for the first moment or two he was walking on the water's
surface just as Jesus was doing, and he didn't sink. But then he
looked around, and he saw the waves, and he felt the wind, and
he thought about the storm, and down he went. So Jesus had to
haul him into the boat and chide him, "You of little faith. . . .
Why did you doubt?" (see Mt 14:22–31). It might have been better if Simon hadn't chanced his faith in that way at all. But that
was Simon.

Then we read of Simon Peter on the mount of transfiguration
with James and John, dazzled while Jesus becomes glowing
white, as the glory of God, the Shekinah, shows itself in him. Simon didn't know what to say, but being Simon he had to say
something. He sees Jesus talking to Moses and Elijah, who had also appeared on the mountain. (Somehow the disciples know who
these visitors are.) So he says to Jesus, "Lord, it is good for us to
be here. If you wish, I will put up three shelters: one for you, one
for Moses and one for Elijah." Again you stand back and scratch
your head and wonder why on earth did he say it? What was the
sense of saying that? Why three shelters rather than one? Why
should any shelters be needed? To keep the sun off or what? Did
Simon want to alert Jesus and Moses and Elijah to the fact that
he could turn his hand to construction if necessary? If so, why?
There is no answer to these questions. Simon makes statements
without asking himself whether they are sensible things to say;
he just says them. That was Simon (see Mt 17:1–8).

And you know how the story of Simon's discipleship before the cross actually ends. It ends with the real spiritual disaster of Simon's denial. Three times he denies that he knows Jesus, that he's ever had anything to do with Jesus, that there's any substance in the idea that he might be a disciple of Jesus. The first two times it was in response to servant girls who said, "I've got a feeling that you're one of Jesus' lot, aren't you?" Simon says twice over, "No, no, no." Then comes the high priest's servant who says, "Didn't I see you in the garden when we arrested this fellow Jesus?" Simon, we're told, now begins to curse and swear and, one imagines, go red in the face and wave his arms, and he insists, "No, I don't know anything about this man." Then he realizes what he's done and is devastated. He went out, we're told, and wept bitterly. And who can wonder? He had said, "Though all the rest of them should disown you, I won't!" But now he hears the cock crow. He realizes that disowning Jesus is precisely what he's done, and he's a broken man.

Thus ends the first act, so to speak, of the three acts of Simon's discipleship story. Simon, as you see, is left very low. His pride is punctured; his self-confidence is gone; he has come apart at the seams. You couldn't have told him at that moment that it was a healthy thing for him that his pride had been punctured and his self confidence taken away, but of course it was, as he himself came to realize in due course.

Have you learned this, I wonder, in your own experience? Until the Lord destroys your self-confidence, he can't do much with you. Sometimes, like Simon Peter we have to make mistakes and actually fail as Christians before that natural self-confidence of ours is destroyed. God in his mercy allows us to fail in order to beat the self-confidence out of us. When he's done that, he can raise us up with a new outlook, trusting him rather than trusting ourselves. That is very healthy for the soul. That, in fact, was the way Jesus was leading Simon.

However, act one of Simon Peter's story closes, as we said, with him devastated and broken and in tears (see Mk 14:66–72; Lk 22:54–62; Jn 18:15–27). He's let his Lord down. The failure is traumatic. In panic he has broken his promise of loyalty in order to save his skin. He feels, and with reason, that what he has done is truly terrible. So Simon, who really had loved Jesus and had meant to be loyal to Jesus, just doesn't know where to put himself—or what to do with himself. I can sympathize, and I hope you can too.

Loyalty with Honesty

In act two we watch Simon Peter in a life-changing encounter with Jesus after the resurrection and just before the ascension. Here we see him recommissioned for that leadership role that he thought he'd forfeited forever by his denial. It is a marvelous manifesting of mercy on the Savior's part. We find the story in John 21.

This is how it all starts: Simon says to his friends, his fellow disciples, "I'm going out to fish." That didn't mean, "I'm going on a fishing vacation," which is what it might mean if you or I used those words. Simon is saying, "I've blown it as far as ministry is concerned. I can't be of service to Jesus anymore, though it breaks my heart to have to admit it. I'm totally disqualified by reason of my public disowning of him. So I'm going back to the old trade. I'm going to be a fisherman again. Will you come with me? We'll fish tonight, we'll catch something, then I can open the shop tomorrow and have something to sell."

This, I suppose, is partly Simon trying to apply balm to his own hurting soul. He knows he is forgiven for his denials. He was one of those whom Jesus commissioned to go and preach him to the world (Jn 20:21–23), but on what seems to him to be mature reflection he feels such a failure that he has to contract out of this vocational enterprise entirely. His natural euphoria and enthusiasm no longer exist, and his credibility (so he feels) is shot. His action shows that he is saying to himself: *I couldn't make it as a disciple, but I can make it as a fisherman. At least I'm good at fishing.* His self-esteem, self-confidence and pride are in ruins, so he plans to give himself an experience of doing what he knows he does well. A psychiatrist would call this a strategy of compensation.

We aren't told what his friends think of his plan, but we see that they're willing to help him. They go out and fish all night. They don't catch anything. Jesus then appears to them on the shore early in the morning and tells them, as he told Simon and his colleagues once before, "Throw the net on the other side of the boat." When they cast the net the way he told them, once again they intercept a shoal of fish and the net is full. So they come to shore and once again they're overawed at the power of the risen Savior, in whose company they're now very glad to be.

Simon, captain of the ship as he was, had already left it. He'd done so in a very Simonish way. There hadn't been any clear thinking behind what he did beyond the fact that he wanted to be the first on shore to greet the Savior. He had grabbed his coverall robe, which he'd taken off for the night's fishing. (They had been working hard and would have been stripped to the waist, and it wouldn't be respectful for him to appear before the Lord stripped to the waist.) So Simon put on his robe. Then he jumps into the water in order to be the first ashore. When he gets to Jesus, he's all wet in every sense of the phrase. It's a good thing that Jesus has lighted a fire so that Simon can huddle by it and dry off.

The story goes on like this. Jesus has made breakfast for them: fish and toasted bread prepared on the fire. (It's quite wonderful how the Savior thinks of our basic human needs, isn't it.) After eating, Jesus takes Simon for a walk along the beach. When they are out of earshot of the other disciples, he says, "Simon, son of John, do you love me more than these?" Jesus' words "more than these," I suppose, are echoing back in his memory to the time when Simon said to him, "Lord, even if all the rest of them disown you, I never will." Of course the threefold denial has intervened between Peter's words then and Jesus speaking to him now, so there is something of a sting in the question, as if Jesus was saying, "Simon, son of John, do you truly love me? Do you imagine you really love me more than these others do?" Simon doesn't make a speech. Wincing at his wretched memories of the denial, he simply says, "Lord, you know that I love you. I know I let myself down dreadfully. I know I was really a traitor to you, Jesus, and I feel horrible at the memory. But Lord, you can read my heart. You know that I love you." There was no guile in Simon: he is being honest and real. Jesus repeats the question a second and third time, and each time Simon gives the same answer.

It has sometimes been doubted whether the third question is really the same as the first two, because John in reporting it uses a different Greek verb for "love." One fairly recent Bible version marks the change by rendering the third question, "Are you my friend?" But this is a false trail; elsewhere in the Gospel, John uses the two verbs as synonyms. The variation is stylistic only. (In any case, Jesus and Simon were almost certainly talking Aramaic, where the difference of nuance that the change of verb is supposed to indicate cannot be expressed by this means.)

The third time Jesus asked the question Simon was hurt, because it seemed to him that Jesus was unwilling to take his word. He couldn't see what his Lord was doing. It's surely obvious that Jesus was inviting him by a threefold profession of love to begin to wash out the bitter memory of that threefold denial. Then each time that Simon said, "Lord, you know that I love you," Jesus immediately gave him a job to do: "Feed my lambs; take care of my sheep; feed my sheep." That was Jesus reinstating Simon in the leadership role in ministry that he had had in mind for his disciple right from the word go. Simon, as we noted, had gone out fishing the night before because he was quite sure that it was all up with his public discipleship and his public ministry. He'd disqualified himself forever from being any use to the Lord Jesus, or so he thought. But here is the Lord Jesus putting him back in that leadership role, specifically recommissioning him for ministry, and the link between Jesus' question to him and the recommissioning is in his words, "Lord, you know that I love you." What Jesus is saying to him is, "Simon, if you really do love me (and I don't doubt your honesty here; I believe you're telling it like it is; I do know what's in your heart)—as one who really does love me, you have got to show it. Love isn't simply a matter of saying that you love; it's a matter of proving that you love by what you do."

That's true across the board, isn't it? Parents show that they love their children, spouses show that they love each other, friends show that they love their friends by what they do for them. Love in the Bible doesn't stop short at words. Love is, in essence, not a feeling of attraction but a purpose of serving by bringing help and benefit. One can love people one does not like, and indeed sometimes we all are required to. So here is Jesus telling Simon, in effect, "Now you've got to show that you love me by action, action very different from the disastrous action that you're remembering. Here the action has got to be that you go out to love and serve and care for and minister to others, specifically to other believers, for my sake. If you love me, then feed my sheep, feed my lambs, take care of the flock, look after these others as my agent and representative." That is Jesus responding to Simon's honesty by restoring him to his ministry. That is Jesus accepting and confirming Simon's profession of love and showing his friend how to demonstrate its genuineness. "Simon, I want you back in my service. Simon, I'm telling you that you are to plan to become a shepherd of my flock. Simon, I want you to be clear that my original purpose for you stands."

Right after that, Jesus pulls aside for a moment the curtain that hides the future. He tells Simon in effect that the disciple is going to finish his ministry by being martyred for the glory of God. I think Jesus did that because he wanted to give Simon an opportunity to negate in an explicit way that panicky passion to save his own skin, which had led to the denial. So Jesus tells him bluntly, "Simon, if you accept my recommissioning, you won't be able to save your skin. I want you to know that. You will glorify me finally by death, a martyr's death, at the hands of the authorities, who will execute you as a subversive, just as they did to me. Now, against the background of that, Simon, I say to you, 'Follow me.'"

Those were Jesus' words to Simon when first he called him to be a disciple (Mt 4:19; compare Jn 1:43). Then the words had meant that Simon must become the peripatetic companion of Jesus, the peripatetic teacher as he traveled to and fro through Galilee and Judea. Now he's using them again. What does he mean by "Follow me" when he is about to leave this world and return to the Father's glory? What he means, clearly, is "Accept my directives, submit to my plans for you, let me guide your

life. Don't duck any of the summonses, challenges, tasks or sufferings that loyalty to me is going to bring upon you. Follow my
leading and my example all the way. Will you commit yourself
to do that, Simon, now that you know what it involves?" You
can see that if Simon says yes, that really does wash out the
paralyzing memory of the denials. Simon would then be saying,
"Lord, I am not going to concern myself with saving my skin
any longer. Yes, I will follow you." Simon understood this, yet
he almost didn't make it.

I suppose that before Simon said anything to Jesus in response, he looked away or stepped aside so that he could have a
moment to think it over. He realized that this was going to be a
big thing to say. He noticed that John was walking along the
beach behind him, and he said to Jesus, "Lord, what about him?
What about John?" He was changing the subject and, for the moment, evading the challenge. But Jesus, in mercy, wouldn't let
him evade the challenge; Jesus says to Simon, "That's nothing to
do with you. What I've got in store for John is neither here nor
there. If it's my will that his life goes on until I come back, that's
none of your business. I am saying to you, Simon, that you (and
the *you* is very emphatic in the Greek) must follow me." Simon
got the message. And the Simon whom we meet in the rest of the
New Testament story is a Simon who is thoroughly committed
(even though he won't be able to save his skin) to following the
Lamb wherever the Lamb leads. So act two sees Simon Peter
spiritually and vocationally restored.

Loyalty with Stability

That leads on to act three of the story, in which Simon Peter
becomes truly and fully the rock, the anchor of the early church.
This section of the story, which opens with the coming of the

Spirit at Pentecost, tells of faithfulness and fruitfulness. Look at the narratives that occupy the first twelve chapters of Acts. In almost every one you see Simon as one way or another God's pioneer, shepherd and anchor man. He is fulfilling the prophecy of his Lord, showing loyalty and love to Jesus by the stability of his commitment and his service.

Right at the end of his life Simon Peter writes two letters to the churches. It's striking to see that stability and steadiness are prominent ideals enforced in both. As we look back over his career and think again of the denial and the foolishness and the failures, we can hardly be surprised that now, as a leader and teacher and apostle seeking to build up the saints, fulfilling a truly apostolic ministry to all sorts and conditions, Simon is concerned about stability.

Here is some of what he writes. First Peter is a letter sent to the churches in the early 60s of the first century, when Christians faced persecution and had to live daily under threat of death. What Peter says to them can be expanded thus, "Be self-controlled and alert. Your enemy the devil prowls around like a roaring lion, looking for someone to devour, just as once he came after me when they arrested Jesus. Jesus' warning about Satan wanting to sift me was dreadfully fulfilled in my denial. Your enemy the devil will be on the lookout for you. Resist him," says Simon Peter, "standing firm in the faith, for you know that your brothers throughout the world are undergoing the same kind of sufferings as you are. And the God of all grace, who called you to his eternal glory in Christ; after you've suffered a little while, will himself restore you and make you strong, firm and steadfast, for whatever faces you after this persecution finishes. Your present sufferings will end, but Satan's attacks on your fidelity will continue as long as life lasts. Prepare to meet them." That's Simon

Peter's call to stability in 1 Peter (see 5:8–11).

Now hear him again in the closing section of 2 Peter. He is talking about Paul's letters, which contain things that are hard to understand, things which, he says, ignorant and unstable people twist and distort, as they do the other Scriptures, to their own destruction. "Don't be like those unstable people," he begs. And he continues: "Therefore, dear friends, since you already know this, be on your guard so that you may not be carried away by the error of lawless men and fall from your secure [or stable] position. But [to ensure that you are not thus carried away and made to fall] grow in the grace and knowledge of our Lord and Savior Jesus Christ. To him be glory both now and forever! Amen" (see 2 Pet 3:15–18). Having experienced something of the spiritual disaster and personal wretchedness into which the devil can plunge the unstable, Simon Peter the pastor is understandably anxious to make sure no one else lapses or collapses that way. So act three of the New Testament story of Simon Peter ends.

Simon Peter in Us

"Everybody loves Peter," said a veteran crosscultural missionary to me. What she meant, I think, was that everybody identifies with a great deal of what they see in Simon Peter: his eager thoughtlessness, his cheerful naive self-confidence, his warm-hearted big brotherliness, his readiness to ask questions when he did not know something and the occasional goofiness of things he blurted out. People empathize too with the depth of his fall when he denied his Lord and with the glory of his restoration as Jesus talked graciously to him at the lakeside and the Holy Spirit came powerfully upon him at Pentecost. They feel, as with Paul, so with Simon Peter, that if God could do so much by way of transforming that man, then there is surely more hope than perhaps they realized for themselves now.

But we need to be honest with ourselves and with God if the hope of God remaking us as he remade Simon is to be fulfilled. Can we say to Jesus with Simon Peter, "Lord, you know that I love you"? No doubt we are compelled to say with him, "Lord, I know I've let you down. What I have done is terrible, and the memory of it is awful—and yet in my heart I do love you, and what I want more than anything is to love you more and better." Have we heard the voice of Jesus speaking pardon and peace to our heart for our sins and failures, and assuring us that despite everything, he still has work for us to do? Have we heard him telling us that the way to show love to anyone, to our Lord himself, to other Christians, to our own nearest and dearest or whomsoever, is by what we do for them, over and above anything we say to them? Becoming thus honest, realistic and responsive to the Son of God was, as we have seen, the path of Simon's progress. It was how he came to know God the Father. It was as he traveled this path that God transformed him from Simon the unstable into Peter the rock. Following this path is in one very basic sense the real apostolic succession. This is the true track for Jesus' true disciples. This is the way you and I must go. May the Lord lead us this way. Let's pray to that end.

Gracious Lord Jesus, we have watched you showing patience and mercy and wonderful restoring grace to Simon, your flawed servant of long ago, whom you turned from being a weak man into a strong man, from being an unstable man into a steady man and from being a weathercock into a rock. In humility, Lord Jesus, we bow before you as those who need that grace which you showed to Simon. Draw near to us Lord Jesus, us who from our hearts tell you that we love you. And work in

*us as you worked in Simon's life for the blessing of others and
the glory of your name. That, Lord Jesus, is our prayer. Grant
it, we beg, and so may your grace and the love of the Father and
the power and the fellowship and the fruitfulness that come
from the Holy Spirit be our portion as long as life shall last. And
so the blessing of Father, Son and Spirit will be upon us. So be
it, Lord. Amen.*

Study

1. What do you see of yourself in Simon Peter?

2. Read John 21. What visual images from this story stand out in your mind?

3. What examples do you see here of Christ's kindness?

4. What evidences do you see of Simon Peter's loyalty to Jesus?

5. If you had been Simon Peter, what would you find difficult about this conversation with Jesus?

6. When have you experienced a time of restoration with God? What continued impact has this restoration had on your life?

7. Read 1 Peter 5:8–11. What changes do these words reflect in Peter's character?

8. What personal encouragement do you find in these closing words to Simon Peter's first letter?

9. As you look back over your own history with Christ, what changes is he making in your character?

10. As a part of his restoration Jesus asked Simon Peter three times, "Do you love me?" How would you answer that question? What specific actions should you take based on your answer?

Pray

■ When other people spoke many different ideas about the identity of Jesus, Simon Peter had these words, "You are the Christ, the Son of the living God" (Mt 16:16). If you are honestly able to do so, pray expressing your commitment to this same faith.

■ At a time when people were leaving Jesus, when Simon Peter may have had good reason to stop following Jesus, he said, "Lord, to whom shall we go? You have the words of eternal life" (Jn 6:68). Meditate on Peter's words as you reflect your own temptations to turn away. Talk to God about your temptations to stray but also about your commitment to him.

■ Simon Peter was a natural leader whom Jesus trained to become a spiritual leader. But he also became a follower—a loyal follower of Jesus. Reflect on the natural abilities to lead and to follow that God has given you. Pray about how he might be refining those abilities as he shapes you into an effective servant in his kingdom.

■ Find a hymn or praise song that expresses your love for Christ. Sing or read it as a prayer.

Write

When Jesus asked Simon Peter the third time, "Do you love me?" his disciple answered, "Lord, you know all things; you know that I love you" (Jn 21:17). Keeping in mind the comfort that God already knows the extent of your love (better even than you know it yourself), reflect on your love for your Lord. Include expressions of your love and commitment to him, any reservations about the extent of your love, and ways that you hope to do the work of showing love to Jesus and to his people.

8

HOPE WHEN EVERYTHING HAS GONE WRONG

Nehemiah

NEHEMIAH WAS A POLITICIAN. FOR MANY YEARS HE WAS A PROvincial governor laboring in Jerusalem as the stated representative of the Persian king, but also and primarily as the servant of his God to make the Jews in Jerusalem into God's holy people. I said he was a politician. I might just as well have said that he was a pastor. We shall see both identities as we explore the thirteenth chapter of his book. Chapter 13 is the end of his personal memoirs. In it Nehemiah tells us what he found when he came back to Jerusalem as governor several years after his first spell had finished and what he did about it.

What Nehemiah found was a great deal that, by God's grace, he had set in order during his first term as governor had gone awry and now had to be put back into shape. This was immensely disappointing for him, although he is so tight-lipped about his feelings that the less-than-thoughtful reader can miss the hints of how acutely distressed he became when he discovered how much had gone wrong. The hints are there, however, in the violence of his restorative actions. Here he describes what he did in order to reestablish things as he knew they should be. In Nehemiah 13:15–22 we read how he restored the sanctifying of the sabbath. Verse 17 tells us that he rebuked the nobles of Judah and said to them, "What is this wicked thing you're doing—desecrating the Sabbath day?" Verses 20 and 21 record how he warned the traders who came to the city and spent the night outside Jerusalem during the Sabbath, hoping to encroach on the seventh day of each week for commercial purposes. "I warned them," says Nehemiah, "and said, 'Why do you spend the night by the wall? If you do this again, I will lay hands on you.' " Tough talk!

That's not all that he did. In the next paragraph (13:23–28) he tells us how he arranged, as in fact he had arranged before (see 10:30; also Ezra 10) but now had to rearrange, the hallowing of home life in Jerusalem. The problem was that Jews had married non-Jews, and their children were now being brought up ignorant of Hebrew, knowing only the pagan language. They were not, therefore, able to understand the teaching and the reading of the Law of God when they were exposed to it. And once again Nehemiah uses strong words. He says (Neh 13:25), "I rebuked them and called curses down on them. I beat some of the men and pulled out their hair." (Strong action too!) "I made them take an oath in God's name and said, 'You are not to give your daughters in marriage to their sons.' "

Then a little further on Nehemiah reminds us of what he had done to provide for the praise of God in Jerusalem. The temple services had been neglected. In 13:4–7 we see that one of Nehemiah's consistent opponents in the past, a man named Tobiah (see Neh 2:10, 19; 4:1-7; 6:1-19), had actually been awarded a private pad in the temple—one of the temple storerooms, in fact—which was scandalous. The reason this could happen was that the tithes that were supposed to come in for the support of the temple servants, the Levites, simply weren't being given, so that the Levites, instead of serving in the temple, had by necessity gone back into the country to work in their own fields. So the storehouse was not being used.

Nehemiah tells us what vigorous steps he took. In 13:8 he says, "I was greatly displeased and threw all Tobiah's household goods out of the room." He gave orders to purify the room, and then he insisted that the tithes and the offerings be brought in henceforth according to the Law of God. Verse 11 says, "I rebuked the officials and asked them, 'Why is the house of God neglected?' " He goes on to tell us in verse 30, "So I purified the priests and the Levites of everything foreign, and assigned them duties each to his own task." In short, he made provision once again for the praise and worship of God as it was meant to be in the temple that he had set in order the first time around (see Neh 10).

We should also notice that this chapter is punctuated with prayers. Nehemiah, concluding his memoirs, inserts the prayers that he made at the time (see Neh 13:14, 22, 29, 30). In the earlier chapters he had sometimes done the same (see 4:4-5; 5:19; 6:14). In 13:22 he prays, "Remember me for this also, O my God, and show mercy to me according to your great love." And then the very last words of the chapter are, "Remember me with favor, O my God."

What now do you make of this man Nehemiah? What do you see in him when you look at the story that he tells us in this closing chapter of his memoirs? Would you enjoy spending an evening with him, do you think? Do you see him as the kind of man whose company you would like to keep? He's a servant of God, that's obvious—and a devoted one too. His service is marked by single-minded intensity. He isn't a man who lets things drift. His mind is very focused. He knows what his goals must be, and he pursues them. He's prepared to do anything within reason to get temple worship back on its feet, to get family life back into shape and to get the sabbath reverently observed in Jerusalem. He knows where he is going, and he takes all steps necessary to that end.

Nehemiah's ministry here is marked, let us also frankly say, by outbursts of anger. He isn't in any sense Mr. Nice Guy. He gets furious with Tobiah and throws all Tobiah's furniture and personal stuff out of the temple room that the Ammonite had been given to occupy. One imagines Tobiah standing by and gibbering while Nehemiah, protected by two or three guards, manhandles the contents of the room with some roughness—or perhaps he stands by Tobiah, studiously ignoring him, directing the guards as they do the evicting. Nehemiah also pulls out the hair of some of the Jewish men who had married pagan women and were bringing up children who couldn't speak Hebrew. That's tough stuff. You see him then as a man of action, not in the least a windbag but a vigorous, even violent agent of change, very worked up about the abuses he is trying to correct.

It just might be that if we were honest we would have to say, "Well, a guy like this is just too strong for me. I can't appreciate that sort of devotion, that sort of service of God. I wonder if God appreciates it! Anyway, I am, or try to be, a gentle man or a gentle woman. Fierce people like Nehemiah are not the sort of company I like to keep."

An Unusual Quality

Was Nehemiah's fury in the temple a moral flaw? For that matter, was Jesus' fury when he cleansed the temple a moral flaw? In an era of political correctness in which tolerating the intolerable is sometimes seen as the highest virtue, it might seem so, but let us think again. We're seeing something in this chapter so rare nowadays that we've hardly got a word for it. And when the regular biblical word for it is used, we hardly know what it means. That word is *zeal*. What we are watching is the action of a zealous servant of God in the face of scandalous irreverence. When you realize that, you begin to wonder, would it have been proper for Nehemiah to react any less vigorously? Would it have been right for Nehemiah to shrug off these things that he found?

Zeal is a quality we meet again and again in Scripture as we read of the Lord and his servants. We meet it when we read how the Lord Jesus made a multi-thonged whip and cleared the temple of the businessmen. The disciples, watching in awe, realized that they were now seeing fulfilled in Jesus what was written in Scripture, "Zeal for your house will consume me" (literally, "eat me up"; see Jn 2:14–17). That's the Lord Jesus, who is our model and our standard in the service of God. And here is Nehemiah showing zeal in a comparable way.

To learn what zeal is, let's take a definition from a real authority, one of the great men of the Church of England at the end of the last century: Bishop J. C. Ryle, first bishop of Liverpool. Listen to the way in which he describes zeal in the chapter that he wrote on the subject. (I ask my women readers not to be offended by his use of the inclusive masculine. Ryle was a Victorian, after all.)

> Zeal in religion is a burning desire to please God, to do his will, and to advance his glory in the world in every possible way. It is a desire

which no man feels by nature—which the Spirit puts in the heart of every believer when he is converted—but which some believers feel so much more strongly than others that they alone deserve to be called "zealous" men. . . . A zealous man in religion is preeminently a man of one thing. It is not enough to say that this person is earnest, hearty, uncompromising, thoroughgoing, wholehearted, fervent in spirit. He only sees one thing, he cares for one thing, he lives for one thing, he is swallowed up in one thing, and that one thing is to please God. Whether this he lives or whether he dies— whether he has health or whether he has sickness—whether he is rich or whether he is poor—whether he pleases men or whether he gives offense—whether he is thought wise or whether he is thought foolish—whether he gets blame or whether he gets praise— whether he gets honor or whether he gets shame—for all this the zealous man cares nothing at all. He burns for one thing; and that one thing is to please God, and to advance God's glory. If he is consumed in the very burning, he cares not for it,—he is content. He feels that, like a lamp, he is made to burn; and if consumed in burning, he has but done the work for which God appointed him. Such a one will always find a sphere for his zeal. If he cannot preach, work and give money, he will cry and sigh and pray. . . . If he cannot fight in the valley with Joshua, he will do the work of Moses, Aaron and Hur on the hill. (Exod. xvii. 9–13 [referring to the work of intercession].) If he is cut off from working himself, he will give the Lord no rest "till help is raised up from another quarter and the work is done. This is what I mean when I speak of "zeal" in religion. (*Practical Religion* [New York: Thomas Y. Crowell, 1959], pp. 130–31)

I'm glad to say that Ryle, who wrote more than a hundred years ago, is not the only person who knows what zeal is. Douglas Rumford has written *Soulshaping* (Wheaton, Ill.: Tyndale, 1996), a fine book on the spiritual life. Right at the end of the book Rumford writes about zeal, pinpointing it as one of the vital signs of a healthy soul. He says,

Zeal should not be confused with emotionalism, extroversion, or even with frenetic activity. It is better described as an unwavering confidence that results in a steady application of the truth of God in life. The person with zeal frequently steps back for renewal and then steps out again in quiet boldness—to share her faith, to stand firm against the temptation to compromise, to go the extra mile when the road is tangled with brambles and brush. . . . Strength comes with the doing of the task. In physical exercise, when you lift weights, the body demands more blood supply to the area where the demand is made. In the process, new circulation routes form, supplying more blood—which means more strength to the area. But if no demand is made, no strength is supplied! If you want to experience spiritual vitality, put yourself in a place where the demand is made on you. For example, bring Jesus Christ into your conversation; say yes to mentoring a young child who has just begun walking with Jesus; reach out to a neighbor in need; pray with a person for healing. Until you step out in faith, your faith will not grow. When you do step out, you will be amazed at your experience of God's presence. It may not—in fact usually does not—come in a dramatic way. But there is a solid peace and confidence that you've done the right thing and God is pleased. (pp. 452–53)

These are words of wisdom and truth. The path of zeal is one that Nehemiah and Jesus and Paul trod, and in this, it seems to me, they set a benchmark and a standard that all believers should aim at. We cannot justify ourselves in not being zealous. We are called to be zealous for our God, as an expression of our love for him, and we don't please him unless we are zealous for him in this way.

Zeal in the New Testament

As was affirmed above, we see this zeal in the Lord Jesus. " 'My food [my meat and drink]' said Jesus, 'is to do the will of him who sent me and to finish his work'" (Jn 4:34). We see it in Paul, coming out in all sorts of things that he says. Here are just two of them, both from the second letter to the Corinthian congregation—a very difficult group to be pastor of, as Paul found. Correcting the notion that his passion for Christ was a sort of lunacy, he says, "Christ's love compels us, because we are convinced that one died for all, and therefore all died. And he died for all, that those who live should no longer live for themselves but for him who died for them and was raised again" (2 Cor 5:14–15). You find Paul again saying, as an expression of his zeal in 2 Corinthians 12:15, "I will very gladly spend for you everything I have and expend myself as well" (spend and be spent for your souls, as the KJV put it). That is not lunacy but jealous love and living zeal. From Paul and Jesus we learn that there is no inconsistency between zeal for the glory of God and love for the people of God. In their hearts both combine, and in Nehemiah's heart the story is the same.

Some of us may find this hard to see. The very ferocity of Nehemiah's zeal makes us think, *Surely this guy is fanatical. He doesn't care for people.* Oh yes, he does, just as Jesus did, just as Paul did. But in love he sought people's good, and you sometimes have to be stern with people if you're going to do them good. Zeal, then, is a Christian virtue that I want to exhort you to seek and to practice.

Nehemiah's Zeal

One of the marks of zealous believers is that they are clear-headed and energetic in pursuing their double goal: the glory of God and the good of souls. Glance back over the story of Nehemiah in the first twelve chapters of his memoir and you will see this in his case. The glory of God through the rebuilding of Jerusalem's walls and the restoring of godliness in the city was Nehemiah's priority throughout. In the first chapter we read how the bad news came that a further attempt to put up the walls of Jerusalem so as to make it once again a defended city had failed. The walls were down; morale was at rock bottom; God was not being honored in the city that bore his name. This news threw Nehemiah into very deep distress. He and his friends prayed for the impossible—that God would grant him mercy in the sight of the man he served; the king of Persia, in others words, would arrange for him to go to Jerusalem himself as governor, the royal representative in that part of the Persian empire, to set things straight.

Nehemiah, the Jew, was nothing more than a high-class slave in the royal palace. There was no slaves' trade union, and the job he was doing for the monarch as the royal cupbearer, which means he was the royal winetaster, was actually a vital job. Winetasters were employed to taste some hours in advance the wine that the big man was going to drink at his evening meal, just in case it was poisoned. From the winetaster's standpoint it was a high-risk occupation; as far as the king was concerned, it was a very necessary and salutary one. So here was Nehemiah, the Jewish slave, winetasting 365 days of the year. How could he hope to get away to do the rebuilding job that his friends had told him he was qualified to tackle? There seemed no possibility of such a thing happening. But Nehemiah believes what his friends have told him, and so he prays, and they pray with him, "Grant me mercy in the sight of this man."

Zeal in Action

As we know, in an amazingly providential way Nehemiah was given permission—indeed a commission—to go to Jerusalem as governor. In fifty-two days, start to finish, he mobilized the inhabitants of Jerusalem and of the land immediately surrounding to rebuild the city wall to a height of probably ten feet and just as thick, with a total length of something like 1.75 miles. After fifty-two days of solid slog, the wall was up. This tremendous achievement called for massive organization. His book records the details of that organization. It was brilliant. But Nehemiah never ascribed success to his organizational skill; the work was done, he wrote, "with the help of our God" (Neh 6:16).

That was not the end. As soon as Jerusalem was walled and safe again, Nehemiah summoned everyone to what we would call a convention day. On that day Ezra and the team of teachers that Ezra had trained taught the law to the whole population. The law had not been taught for generations. The people simply did not know how to serve God. But God poured out his Spirit and there was something of a revival. When their God, who had given them back their city, was revealed to them as the God who had a code, a moral law, standards, constant requirements, the impact was such that they broke down. They wept. The teaching had to stop.

Then Nehemiah, in his role as the day's emcee, said to them, "Okay, that's all we can handle for now. Go and feast. Go and rejoice. Remember, the joy of the Lord is your strength" (see Neh 8:9–12). That was a secret that Nehemiah himself had proved in the course of building the wall. Such was Nehemiah's performance. If Moses was the first founder of Israel under God, Nehemiah was the second.

This was zeal showing itself in action. This was active service of God, as active service of God should be. If we ask, "Why should anyone be passionate about serving God in the way that Nehemiah was passionate about serving God?" Paul answers us in the words quoted from 2 Corinthians 5:14, "Christ's love compels us."

Zeal in Prayer

Now note how, all the way through Nehemiah's book, his prayers run. He is a man of prayer, as we saw from the prayers he inserted in chapter 13. It seems that from the start, at every turn of the road, he turned to prayer—and he led others to turn to prayer. In 4:8–9 he tells us about the plot that had been formed to flatten the wall that he was beginning to put up. An alliance of enemies (including Tobiah, by the way) all plotted together to come and fight against Jerusalem, but Nehemiah tells us, "We prayed to our God." That was the first response. Then we "posted a guard day and night to meet this threat."

Pray first and commit your cause to God. Pray first and take the steps that seem appropriate. Pray first and let God guide you in what to do in the crisis. Nehemiah understood that principle and practiced it. When the little gang of enemies were trying to persuade him to panic, hoping Israel's hands would then get weak so that the work on the wall would not be completed, "they were all trying to frighten us," says Nehemiah, "but I prayed, 'now strengthen my hands'" (Neh 6:9). And God did. The prayers that you find in the thirteenth chapter are the last in the long series of recorded prayers of God's servant. Nehemiah wasn't self-reliant; he was God-reliant. He rejoiced in the faithfulness of God and trusted and prayed. The joy of the Lord and the subjective fruit of his prayer was his strength.

Zeal in Mission

As the late great C. T. Studd, pioneer missionary in China and India and Africa (yes, all three countries), once said, "If Jesus Christ be God and died for me, no sacrifice is too great for me to make for him." Zeal in the service of the Lord matches the greatness of the Lord's love in our redemption. It's obvious, isn't it? Those who have been greatly loved should love greatly and serve zealously in return. We sing, "Love so amazing, so divine, demands my soul, my life, my all." We are right.

C. T. Studd used the word *sacrifice*. His point was that there's always something that has to be left behind if you're going to embrace God's vocation for you. One rather portentous but nonetheless very profound way of expressing this is to say the Christian life according to the New Testament is to be lived according to the baptismal pattern, which means that experiences of renunciation even to death (or what feels like death) constantly precede experiences of resurrection in which you're made rich again. But the resurrection doesn't come until after the death. And it's round the circle of that pattern for each of us over and over again: death followed by resurrection is the recurring sequence. This is part of the Lord's discipline for our personal living, just as it's part of the pattern of the Lord's work in the church and in the world. People like C. T. Studd understood this.

People like Paul have understood it too. The hymn that Paul quotes in Philippians 2:6–11 says that Jesus Christ did not see equality with God as something to hang onto, but emptied himself of it, gave it up and took on human form, coming to this world as a man, a poor man, indeed as a slave, who ended up hanging in agony on the cross for our redemption. Such was the love of Christ. If we can get that love clear in our minds, we'll see the force of C. T. Studd's reasoning. "If Jesus Christ be God and died for me, then no sacrifice is too great for me to make for him." Unanswerable!

Nehemiah I think would tell us, if he were here to testify (and so would the apostle Paul, and so do I from the little I know about it) that zealous, single-minded service of God doesn't feel like sacrifice when you're engaged in it. It feels, rather, like active gratitude, seeking self-expression in active faithfulness. It feels, indeed, like living the life that you were meant to live and that the Lord redeemed you for. Have we, I wonder, all seen this?

Have we started to seek the grace of zeal for our life with our Lord?

Let me give you a couple of examples of zeal. George White-field, the eighteenth-century evangelist, was a Nehemiah-like pioneer. In the British evangelical revival usually associated with Wesley, Whitefield set everything going. I have a special interest in George Whitefield. I was privileged to go to his old school in Gloucester, England, and, insofar as anyone has ever been my role model, it's been Whitefield. Whitefield for years and years, as his amazed friend Henry Venn tells us, used to work an eighty-hour week, preaching up to twenty-five one- to two-hour sermons and expounding the Scriptures, with prayer and singing, in many private houses. He never seemed to feel weary; he loved doing it. He knew he'd been greatly loved by Jesus, and he loved serving the Savior and showing his gratitude.

The Lord gave George Whitefield incredible strength and incredible freshness for his thirty-five years of ministry before, finally spent, he was taken home in his middle fifties. He had said he would rather burn out than rust out, and so he did. But that's zeal. That's how the Lord will use a zealous man. Whitefield was the lightning rod of renewal on both sides of the Atlantic for almost a complete generation. He's a man whom I much admire and often think of, as I do Nehemiah.

I can also tell you about a Canadian, of whom I speak as a Britisher by genes who is now a Canadian by choice. Have you ever heard of Jonathan Goforth, pioneer missionary in China at the end of the nineteenth century, agent of God in revival in various parts of the Chinese church? When Jonathan Goforth proposed to the English lady whom he hoped to marry and who later wrote his biography, he said, "Will you give me your promise that always you will allow me to put my Lord and his work first, even

before you?" Writing his biography forty-seven years after, she
frankly admitted that she hesitated at the time before she said
yes. But having been his life partner in evangelistic and pastoral
mission in China for more than a generation, she testified that
she was very glad she did.

These are single examples; more could be cited, but these suf-
fice to make our point. Remember Christ. Remember Nehemiah.
Remember Paul. Remember George Whitefield. Remember
Jonathan Goforth. Remember C. T. Studd. And never be lacking
in zeal. You can't always be Mr. or Ms. Nice Guy if you're going to
be zealous and faithful in the service of your Lord. But it's right,
proper and required that you and I be zealous and faithful in that
service, whatever the cost and whatever the offense.

Zeal in Us

Thus far I have been commending and applauding zeal as a
Christian virtue and urging that we seek it for each day's living. I
need to say, however, that with zeal comes risk—the risk of well-
meant wildness and perversity. Passionate living, of which zeal
for God is one very noble form, easily becomes unbalanced,
fanatical and obsessive, marked by tunnel vision and all sorts of
unwisdom that its cool, detached, grooved, sluggish opposite will
avoid. Today's light-hearted society knows this well and is alter-
nately amused by and suspicious of passionate seriousness about
anything.

Nehemiah, the zealous leader, motivator and manager, seems
not to have failed at any stage in either breadth of vision or skill
in management; yet we cannot help wondering whether he needed to be quite so fierce in the way he evicted Tobiah from the
temple precincts, or threatened violence to sabbath traders, or
beat and cursed and tore at the hair of Jewish men with pagan

families. Clearly, from the way he tells his story, he thought he needed to be this fierce, and maybe he did if the deformed community was ever to get back into shape. None of us can be sure, for we were not there.

All the same, as I said, we cannot help wondering. Certainly we who aspire to zeal need constantly to consult with prudent peers regarding what we hope to do lest we miss the path of wisdom. We need also to have it clear in our minds that violence, whether emotional, verbal or physical, while easily stirred up by zeal in our im-perfectly sanctified hearts and sometimes necessary as a means to an end, must ever be minimal in ministry. Zeal that is needlessly rude and rough with people is to that extent unspiritual. Zeal that, however firm and strong in its endeavors, is as gentle and restrained as possible in dealing with our fellow humans is thereby revealed as an expression of love to God and neighbor, which is how it should be. That is the sort of zeal we are to seek.

Furthermore, in light of the story in Nehemiah 13 it needs to be said specifically that disappointment must not be allowed in any way to diminish our zeal for the honor and work of God. Whatever happens, we must keep our priorities in place and look to God as steadily as we can to ensure that our energy in pursuing them, even if temporarily lessened, will not be permanently reduced. This is important, for we all have our disappointments from time to time (finding we have wasted our input and labor, or been let down, or deceived, or denied justice, or been disabled, or penalized, or have lost someone or something that we valued enormously, or had our hopes dashed some other way). Nehemiah, we may be sure, felt tremendous disappointment when he found that so much of the good and godly order that had come out of the wall building and the revival during his first spell as governor (Neh 9—10) had now fallen by the wayside. Nonetheless, he does not see the situation as beyond hope and zealously sets himself for the second time to rebuild God-honoring life in Jerusalem.

The book of Ecclesiastes spends chapter after chapter pointing out that life is full of disappointments, situations of frustration and waste and tragedy that "under the sun" seem to make no sense. Nonetheless, the book ends on an upbeat note of hope that is very positive, even if not very informative. Having stated that the whole business of life is to fear God and keep his commandments, the writer declares: "For God will bring every deed into judgment, including every hidden thing, whether it is good or evil" (Eccles 12:14). Judgment, we must remember, is for approbation and reward, as well as for retribution upon wrongdoers; this is Ecclesiastes's low-key way of expressing what Paul passionately articulates in his admonition to the Corinthians: "Therefore, my dear brothers, stand firm. Let nothing move you. Always give yourselves fully to the work of the Lord, because you know that your labor in the Lord is not in vain" (1 Cor 15:58). God's people are never left without hope, even if it seems that everything around us has gone wrong. In God's sight all faithful endeavor has lasting value, even when humanly it appears to have been fruitless. So we must never be found less than zealous in living for the Lord we serve and love.

So maybe you and I need to reorder our public image and our self-image a little bit so that we have a different goal than always to appear in public as a "nice" person. What's important is that we should appear in public not necessarily as compliant, tolerant, jolly persons but as faithful and zealous ones. Sometimes we shall be up against things that call for quite strong words and quite vigorous action. We won't be loved for speaking those words or taking that action—just as Jesus, in the short term, wasn't loved for clearing the temple. But faithfulness to his Father required it. And faithfulness to our heavenly Father is going to require of us from time to time that we say in our hearts, *Never mind what they think. This is what I ought to be saying; this is what I ought to be doing; I know I should; so Lord help me and I will.*

I won't say that this is the heroic side of the Christian life. *Heroism* really is the wrong word, because heroism implies that you do what you do drawing on your own resources, and service of the Lord Jesus should never be that. Nehemiah, when asked by the king what it was that was troubling him, prayed before he spoke (Neh 2:4–5). Arrow prayers, as we call them, only take about a second to offer, but they make a tremendous difference to what happens. You and I should also get into the habit of firing off arrow prayers to our God when something that is difficult to say, difficult to do, or something that's going to get us into hot water in the short term nonetheless has to be said or done. That's the pattern we see in Nehemiah, and that's the way we are to go.

God, give us zeal. God, move us to seek zeal. God, prompt us to take Nehemiah and Paul and Jesus as role models in zeal. God, prompt us to take to heart what Paul says in Romans 12:11, "Never be lacking in zeal." This is as explicit and as strong as a command can be. If ever we find our zeal sagging, may God give us grace to look back to the cross and to brood a little on the greatness of God's love, the greatness of God's faithfulness, the overwhelming reality that Christ died for our sins to save us, renew us, give us our new life here and our hope of glory hereafter, and I believe our zeal will return to us. We'll go on our way rejoicing in the strength of the Lord to be zealous once more for him.

Gracious Heavenly Father, we the halfhearted, convicted by your word of our halfheartedness, bow low before your throne, for that is the only way in which, as the guilty halfhearted, we can truly lift up our hearts to you. We have to humble ourselves and acknowledge our halfheartedness, pray for forgiveness and seek from you the grace to be zealous. And we beg, our Father, that we shall never again dishonor you and seem to make light of Jesus our Savior by being casual, halfhearted, unfocused at a deep level, unconcerned about the praise of Jesus in our life and service. Love so amazing, so divine, demands our life, our soul, our all. So we tell you that your amazing love in our redemption shall have our life and soul and all that we are. And by your grace we will seek to practice zeal, to show forth zeal and to serve with zeal at all times everywhere. Make us single-minded to love you and to love others with all our might. Grant it, Lord, in Jesus' name. Amen.

Study

1. Read Nehemiah 13. In what ways did Nehemiah show himself to be a person of zeal?

2. What would be hard about living under Nehemiah's leadership during this time? What would be good about it?

3. Reread the last three paragraphs before the subheading "An Unusual Quality" (pp. 163-65). How would you describe your own level of comfort with a person who is truly zealous?

4. In what ways would you like to be more like Nehemiah?

5. Four times in Nehemiah 13, Nehemiah interrupts his narrative to pray (see verses 14, 22, 29, 30). What do these prayers suggest about his character?

6. What value do you see to this kind of praying?

7. George Whitefield is one to "follow . . . even though very far behind." Of what zealous Christian would you like to make a similar statement of your own? Why?

8. "Zealous, single-minded service to God doesn't feel like sacrifice when you are doing it. It feels like gratitude." To what extent have you seen or experienced this? How does this statement challenge you?

9. How could you begin to develop and appropriate zeal for God?

10. What might be some natural and appropriate ways for you to express that zeal?

Pray

■ Nehemiah prayed (13:22), "Remember me for this also, O my God, and show mercy to me according to your great love." Prayerfully consider what you would like God to remember you for. You could begin by praying, "Remember me when . . ." Then talk with God about those memories—the good and the bad. There is no need to brag or to be self-deprecating. When appropriate, pause and ask that God remember you in mercy.

■ In Nehemiah 8:10, when the people were overcome by their sin, Nehemiah instructed, "Do not grieve, for the joy of the LORD is your strength." Pray about some of the things that grieve you. But as you pray, allow yourself to rejoice in God's strength.

■ "If ever we find our zeal sagging, God give us grace to look back to the cross and to brood a little on the greatness of God's love, the greatness of God's faithfulness, the overwhelming reality that Christ died for our sins." Use the words of the great hymn "When I Survey the Wondrous Cross" to meditate and pray about Christ's gift on the cross—and your zeal for him.

When I survey the wondrous cross
On which the Prince of glory died,
My richest gain I count but loss,
And pour contempt on all my pride.

Forbid it, Lord, that I should boast,
Save in the death of Christ, my God;
All the vain things that charm me most,
I sacrifice them to his blood.

See, from his head, his hands, his feet,
Sorrow and love flow mingled down;

Did e'er such love and sorrow meet,
Or thorns compose so rich a crown?

Were the whole realm of nature mine,
That were an offering far too small;
Love so amazing, so divine,
Demands my soul, my life, my all.

—Isaac Watts, 1707, 1709

Write

Reflect on paper about your zeal for your Lord. When have you been
overzealous, perhaps for the wrong motive or the wrong cause? When has
your zeal brought potential harm? Write also about those times when
your zeal has been (or is) low. Think on paper about how you can serve
your Lord with holy zeal.